THE TRAGEDY OF Othello

THE MOOR OF VENICE

EDITED BY
George Lyman Kittredge

Revised by Irving Ribner

THE TRAGEDY OF

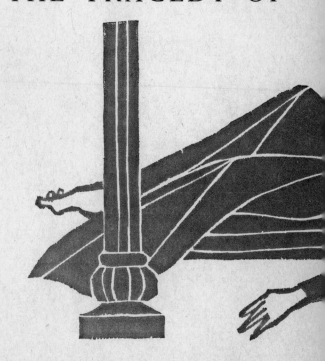

William Shakespeare

Othello

The Moor of Venice

John Wiley & Sons, Inc.

New York · London · Sydney · Toronto

ISBN 0 471 00525 8

LIBRARY OF CONGRESS CATALOG CARD NUMBER: 66-30754

PRINTED IN THE UNITED STATES OF AMERICA.

10 9 8 7

PREFACE

The New Kittredge Shakespeares

The publication of George Lyman Kittredge's *Complete Works of Shakespeare* in 1936 was a landmark in Shakespeare scholarship. The teacher who for almost half a century had dominated and shaped the direction of Shakespearean study in America produced what was recognized widely as the finest edition of Shakespeare up to his time. In the preface to this edition Kittredge indicated his editorial principles; these allowed a paramount authority to the Folio of 1623 and countenanced few departures from it while, at the same time, refusing to "canonize the heedless type-setters of the Elizabethan printing house." Kittredge's work was marked by a judicious conservatism and a common sense rarely found in equal measure in earlier editors of Shakespeare. In the thirty-odd years which have gone by since the appearance of this monumental volume, however, considerable advances have been made in the establishment of Shakespeare's text, and our body of knowledge about the dates, sources, and general historical background of Shakespeare's plays has vastly increased. The present revision is designed to apply this new knowledge to Kittredge's work so that it may have as much value to the student and general reader of today as it had to those of thirty years ago.

Before his death Kittredge had issued, in addition to *The Complete Works*, separate editions of sixteen of the plays, each copiously annotated. Some of the notes were unusually elaborate, but they interpreted Shakespeare's language with a fullness and precision attained by few other commentators, for Kittredge had few equals in his intimate knowledge of Elizabethan English. In freshly annotating the plays I have, accordingly, tried to use Kittredge's own notes as fully as space would permit. Where I have repeated his distinctive language or recorded his characteristic critical opinions, I have followed the note with the symbol [к]; where Kittredge's definition of a term can be found in essentially the same words in other editions, I have not used the identifying symbol. Every annotator draws upon the full body of the notes of earlier editors, and to give credit for every note is impossible. Notes have been placed at page bottoms.

The brief introductions which Kittredge wrote for the plays have been replaced by new ones, for what seemed like indisputable fact some thirty years ago often appears today to be much more uncertain, and many new issues of which Kittredge was not aware have been raised in recent criticism. The new introductions seek to present what are now generally agreed to be basic facts about the plays and to give some indications of the directions which modern criticism has taken, although specific analyses of individual plays are avoided.

Such great authority attaches to Kittredge's text that it has not frequently — and never lightly — been departed from. Where changes have been made, they have usually involved the restoration of copy-text readings now generally accepted in place of the emendations of eighteenth- and nineteenth-century editors of which Kittredge, in spite of his extraordinary conservatism in this regard, sometimes too easily approved. Only rarely has an emendation been adopted in the present revision which was not also adopted by Kittredge. All departures from the copy-texts are indicated in the notes, emendations followed by the names of the editors by whom they were first proposed. Wherever Kittredge's text has been departed from for any reason, his reading is given in the notes. Modern spelling has in a few instances been substituted for Elizabethan forms which are mere spelling variations but which Kittredge nevertheless retained. His punctuation has not been altered except in a few very rare instances.

The system of recording elisions and contractions which Kittredge explained in his introduction to *The Complete Works* has been retained, as has his method of preserving to the fullest the copy-text stage directions, with all additions to them enclosed within square brackets. Although modern editors recognize the vagueness of the place settings of Elizabethan plays and are reluctant to include the place designations so favoured by eighteenth- and nineteenth-century editors, much historical interest nevertheless attaches to these, and Kittredge's place designations accordingly have been retained between square brackets. Kittredge's attempt to retain the line numbering of the Globe text, which resulted in considerable irregularity in prose passages, has been abandoned, and the lines of each play have been freshly numbered. Kittredge's act and scene divisions have been retained, as has his practice of surrounding by square brackets those divisions which are not in the copy-texts.

The *New Kittredge Shakespeares* include individual editions of each of the plays, the sonnets, and the minor poems, and a new edition of *The Complete Works* in a single volume. A comprehensive introduction to Shakespeare's life, times, and theatrical milieu is available both as a separate volume and as an introduction to *The Complete Works*.

IRVING RIBNER

INTRODUCTION

The Tragedy of Othello,
The Moor of Venice

◇◇◇◇◇
◇◇◇◇◇ On November 1, 1604, Shakespeare's company, the
◇◇◇◇◇ King's Men, performed "The Moor of Venis" by "Shax-
berd" before King James I and his court at Whitehall. This performance is reported in the "Revels Accounts" printed by Peter
Cunningham in 1842. Although the authenticity of these accounts was for a long time disputed, and Cunningham in some
quarters accused of forgery, this unfair charge has long since
been disposed of, and no one today seriously doubts that the
accounts are genuine. It is impossible to say precisely, however,
just when *Othello* was written. General considerations of style
and structure would indicate that the play followed soon after
Hamlet. In the "bad quarto" of *Hamlet,* produced by memorial
reconstruction in 1603, there are echoes of *Othello,* which would
indicate that the actors reproducing *Hamlet* had played in
Othello as well. There appears also to be an echo of *Othello* in
the line "more savage than a barbarous Moor" in *Part I* of *The
Honest Whore* written by Dekker and Middleton before March
14, 1604. The best guess seems to be that *Othello* was written
in late 1601 or 1602 and that it had been performed upon the
public stage before the court performance recorded in the
"Revels Accounts."

TEXT

Othello was never printed during Shakespeare's lifetime. On
October 6, 1621, it was entered in the Stationers' Register for
Thomas Walkley, and it was printed for him in quarto (Q¹) by
Nicholas Okes in 1622. In the following year it was included in

the First Folio (F^1) in a version some 160 lines greater in length. The relation of these two substantive texts to one another has been much disputed and provides a problem for editors. It is today generally believed that Q^1 was set up from a transcript of a shortened version of the play probably prepared for performance in the provinces, and that F^1 was set up from a copy of Q^1, which had been corrected and filled in marginally by reference to a fuller version of the play, either a transcript of Shakespeare's original manuscript (foul papers) or the original theatre prompt-book. Nevill Coghill (*Shakespeare's Professional Skills*, Cambridge: Cambridge University Press, 1964, pp. 164–202) has recently suggested, however, on the basis of the dramatic quality of the F^1 additions, that Q^1 may represent Shakespeare's original version of the play and that F^1 may represent his own revision, after the play had had some experience on the stage, for the sake of greater dramatic effectiveness. The theory is an attractive one, although extremely difficult to substantiate.

The F^1 text, which is divided into acts and scenes, has always been regarded by editors as the superior of the two texts, because it preserves important additions to the play and because most of its variations from Q^1 represent the careful correction of errors by reference to a highly authoritative manuscript. It is, accordingly, followed in the present edition. The F^1 text, however, is contaminated by Q^1 errors that have been carried over into it, by a fairly large number of compositor's errors, as well as by the attempts of an expurgator to remove profanity from the play. The readings of Q^1, which has considerable independent authority, have therefore been preserved whenever they seem clearly preferable to those of F^1. Any edition of *Othello* must be an eclectic one; here the seldom erring judgment of Kittredge has been heavily relied upon. Because the variants between the two texts are very numerous, many being mere accidentals of slight significance, only those Q^1 readings about which there has been significant critical controversy have been recorded in the notes, as are all departures from Kittredge's text. A second quarto (Q^2), printed in 1630, has no independent authority, because it was set up from a copy of Q^1 corrected by reference to F^1. A third quarto (Q^3), printed in 1655, is merely a reprint of Q^2.

The following passages are omitted in the Q^1 text: I.1.120–36;

I.ii.65, 72–7; I.iii.24–30; II.iii.3, 261–3. ("Drunk . . . shadow");
III.iii.383–90 ("By the world . . . satisfied"), 453–60 ("Iago . . .
heaven"); IV.i.37–43 ("To confess . . . devil"); IV.ii.151–64
("Here . . . make me"); IV.iii.30–51 ("I have . . . next"), 53–5,
58–61, 84–102; V.ii.151–4, 185–93, 246–8 ("What . . . willow"),
266–72.

GIRALDI CINTHIO

Shakespeare found the story of *Othello* in the seventh *novella* of
the third day of the *Hecatommithi* of Giovanni Battista Giraldi
Cinthio, published in Venice in 1566 and not translated into
English until 1753, although a French translation by Gabriel
Chappuys was printed in Paris in 1584. We cannot be certain
whether Shakespeare read the story in the Italian or the French,
but a close comparison of the play with both versions makes it
far more likely that it was based upon the Italian, which Shakespeare presumably was able to read. Giraldi Cinthio was himself
a dramatist of considerable importance, being among the very
first to apply the techniques of Senecan tragedy to the matter of
contemporary everyday life. His plays are usually based upon
the very prose stories he included in his collection *Hecatommithi*,
and these reveal his journalistic proclivities, for they are often
based upon actual recent events of sensational interest. The relation of *Othello* to the tradition of "domestic tragedy" reflected
in Thomas Heywood's *A Woman Killed with Kindness* may owe
something to the origin of the story in Cinthio's narrative.

The story of *Othello* appears to have been based upon an actual murder of rather sordid nature that took place in Venice
around 1508. In Cinthio's account only Desdemona is named
(Disdemona); Othello is simply called "the Moor" (*il Moro*);
Iago is the "ensign" (*alfiero*), and Cassio is the captain of a company (*capo di squadra*). Kittredge has neatly summarized the
tale as Cinthio tells it:

> In the novel we are told briefly that the Moor is highly regarded
> by the lords of Venice for his valour and his military genius, and
> that they appoint him commander of the troops they are sending
> to Cyprus. He has married a Venetian lady who had fallen in love
> with him because of his *virtù*, but no account is given of his won-

derful adventures. . . . The ensign is not a disappointed candidate
for Cassio's place. He has conceived a violent passion for Disdemona
and thinks that her coldness is due to her love for the *capo di
squadra,* with whom he believes she is carrying on an intrigue. His
love turns to hatred. The *capo di squadra* is cashiered by the Moor
for disorderly conduct on guard and for beating a soldier, and
Disdemona urges her husband to reinstate him. The ensign, to con-
vince the Moor of Disdemona's guilt, declares that the *capo* has
boasted to him of his success. The handkerchief is stolen by [the
ensign while Disdemona dandles his little child on her lap], and
is dropped by him in the *capo's* lodging. The Moor and the ensign
agree that Disdemona and her supposed lover must die. The ensign
attacks the *capo,* but does not succeed in killing him. The Moor
asks the ensign's advice. "Shall Disdemona be poisoned, or shall
she be killed with a knife?" He replies that he has thought of a
better way: "The ceiling of your chamber is badly cracked. Let us
beat her to death with a stocking filled with sand, so that no
bruises may show. Then we will pull down the ceiling and pretend
that a beam has fallen upon her head. Everybody will think her
death an accident." The plan is successfully carried out; but the
Moor, who loved Disdemona "more than his eyes," runs mad with
grief and rushes about, searching for her everywhere in the house.
He deprives the ensign of his office and they become bitter enemies.
The Moor, whom the ensign accuses of the murder, is tortured by
the Venetian authorities, but will not confess. He is condemned to
lifelong exile and is finally killed by Disdemona's relatives. The
ensign is not suspected. Later, however, he dies under torture to
which he has been subject in connection with another affair. After
his death his wife reveals the whole truth about the murder.

   Cinthio was a deliberate moralist; most of the tales in his collection were *exempla* designed to teach simple moral lessons re-
lated to domestic affairs. This particular story he told as a
warning to parents to look well to the disposal of their daughters
in marriage, to warn of what might happen to a girl who married a man of different race, religion, and social customs (*la
natura, il Cielo, la modo della vita*). The story of a brutal murder of a wife with a sandbag would seem to offer little scope for
tragedy, but the moral lesson of Cinthio had stressed certain
elements upon which Shakespeare's imagination worked, most

notably the seeming unnaturalness of the marriage and the alien-
ation of Othello from Venetian society, which become integrating
themes of crucial importance in his play.

EVIL AS DECEPTION

Kittredge has written that "*Othello* is, in plan and structure,
that rare phenomenon in literature — a tragedy in which the
hero is passive (or acted upon) and the force that opposes him
(the villain of the piece) is the power that sways him until the
turning point." Othello is the tragic hero who is honestly deceived, who chooses evil under the delusion that it is good because he has been so worked upon that he has been rendered
incapable of distinguishing appearance from reality, truth from
falsehood. To create this situation Shakespeare uses the theme of
unnaturalness he had found in Cinthio. For a noble Venetian
lady to marry a black alien would have been as shocking to
Shakespeare's audience as it was to Cinthio's readers, and many
may have wondered with Brabantio whether Othello had indeed
used drugs to attain his ends. Shakespeare dwells upon the seeming unnaturalness of the marriage, stressing the colour of Othello
and his strangeness beyond anything in Cinthio's tale, while at
the same time he keeps before the audience the selfless affection,
devoid of sexual passion, which has led to the marriage, affirming
that what in its outward appearance seems strange and unnatural
is in reality pure and good. Black was a traditional sign of
lechery, going back to the Middle Ages, and it was the colour of
the Devil. In Shakespeare's play the outward appearance of evil
and lechery covers an inward nobility and purity. To this reality
Desdemona had responded in choosing Othello: "I saw Othello's
visage in his mind" (I.iii.252).

In the same manner Iago, outwardly white, is inwardly black.
To all the world, and most notably to Othello, he is "Honest
Iago," but he reveals himself in the very first scene as a creature
of evil and deception: "I am not what I am" (I.i.65). Honesty to
Elizabethans meant chastity, but Iago is a creature who equates
love with lust and who is himself torn by a groundless sexual
jealousy of his wife. Iago is evil disguised as good, and in this
role he works upon Othello, using his strangeness, his idealism

and sense of honour, his unfamiliarity with women, and his consciousness of his position as an alien in an always potentially hostile society; he causes Othello to see his own marriage as Iago sees it: an unnatural union between an "erring barbarian and a supersubtle Venetian" (I.III.353) whose result can only be the sordid cuckolding of the husband. The action of the play involves the process by which Othello, seduced by evil wearing the mask of good, comes to see the world through the eyes of Iago. He is thus transformed from a noble soldier into an inhuman monster, and in this guise, regarding the most brutal and pathetic of crimes as an act of justice demanded by honour, he murders the wife who has loved him beyond all other considerations and who with her dying breath attempts to shield his crime from discovery.

MOTIVATION AND CREDIBILITY

Thomas Rymer in his *Short View of Tragedy* (1692) criticized *Othello* as "plainly none other, than a Bloody Farce, without salt or savour," whose moral "may be a warning to all good Wives, that they look well to their Linen." This view, which is in fact quite consistent with the critical premises of the late seventeenth century, has been subjected to much ridicule, but Rymer was in fact reacting against what has bothered succeeding generations of critics: the seeming incredibility of the heroic Othello's fall before the petty trickery of Iago and Iago's own apparent lack of motivation.

E. E. Stoll has suggested that Shakespeare deliberately removed from the play those elements in his source which might have more readily explained Othello's downfall, and that he did so in the interest of "steep tragic contrast" — to shock his audience by the spectacle of a character performing an act that the audience has been led to believe him, by every element in his characterization, incapable of performing. But Shakespeare is interested in effects more profound than those of simple shock. Within the ideational framework of the play Othello must be seen as a man capable of succumbing to evil through wrong moral choice, as all men are capable. But Shakespeare has nevertheless drawn him, as Kittredge has perceived, in naturalistic

terms by which his fall is sufficiently explained for the purposes
of the play:

> Othello is a Moorish noble of royal lineage (I.ii.21–24) who has
> lived an adventurous life. He is not a Mohammedan, however, but
> a Christian. Shakespeare conceives him as an Oriental (and there-
> fore as a man of naturally impetuous temper) who has achieved
> self-control (III.iv.127–34). But this fortitude of mind breaks down
> under the stress to which he is subjected. He has a frank and open
> nature and is "not easily jealous" — for we must accept what Shake-
> speare makes him say of himself in the manifestly expository pas-
> sage at the end of the play. Thus he is helpless in the hands of a
> man like Iago, as Gloucester is helpless in the hands of Edmund.
> So his words to Emilia bear witness, at the very acme of the tragic
> climax, when revelation is at hand: "My friend, thy husband:
> honest, honest Iago."

But although Shakespeare has drawn a man whose fall is credible,
it is not inevitable or fated; Othello falls through his own free
moral choice.

Samuel Taylor Coleridge in a famous passage spoke of Iago's
soliloquies as "the motive-hunting of motiveless malignity." It is
a brilliant observation, but it is only partly true. Within the
general thematic framework of the play Iago needs no more
motivation than the Devil needs to tempt man. Although he is
not to be viewed as the Devil in human form, as some critics
have indeed seen him, he is plainly cast as a symbol of evil whose
very nature it is to corrupt his fellow man. But he too is cast in
naturalistic terms that do not conflict with his symbolic function; indeed he represents one of Shakespeare's supreme triumphs
in realistic character portraiture. The human Iago and the realistic psychology upon which Shakespeare has grounded his villainy are again well described by Kittredge:

> In fact, Iago's initial motive is set forth with passionate vigour.
> He is actuated by resentment for injustice, and there are few mo-
> tives to which men so instantly respond. Cassio has the place which
> Iago expected and to which, so far as we can weigh their merits,
> he seems to have had the better claim. At all events, Cassio's be-
> haviour in his office is far from meritorious and Iago's military
> record is unassailable. Iago feels all the practical soldier's contempt

for the technical theorist. There is further ground for resentment
in the fact that Cassio is a foreigner — "one Michael Cassio, a
Florentine," one of a tribe of bankers and bookkeepers, whose
very princes were merchants. There is no difficulty, then, in finding
a motive for Iago, and (what is vital in every tragic action) this
motive is not only human (that is, neither monstrous nor maniacal),
but has a kind of foundation in reason and justice. In Iago's can-
kered nature resentment for real or fancied injury brought with it
boundless possibilities of crime. But Shakespeare has combined
with this the motive that he found in Cinthio — lust (II.1.285); and
to this he has added the suspicion that Othello is Emilia's lover.
This last is not a mere pretense; it is a raging torment —

> the thought whereof
> Doth, like a poisonous mineral, gnaw my inwards.

It is a common error to assume that Iago's whole course of villainy is deliberate. Until the end of the first act he has no definite
scheme in mind — only a general desire to be revenged. His plans
take shape gradually, and their progress is carefully indicated. He
is a deliberate opportunist and he modifies them to fit each emer-
gency. His wish is to supplant Cassio and to torment Othello, but
he contemplates no tragic issue; nor is it clear to him until the
third scene of Act III that both Cassio and Desdemona must die.
Nothing else can prevent the exposure of his perfidy.

Thus Iago, along with Othello and Desdemona, becomes the
victim of his own villainy; he is destroyed by the very evil he
brings into being.

THE PROBLEM OF TIME

The many inconsistencies and improbabilities in the action of
Othello tend to be obscured by the heightened intensity and the
rapid movement of the play. Audiences in the theatre rarely have
any awareness of problems that are raised by the reader in his
study. Among these is the problem of time, for a close reading of
the text reveals that not enough time has elapsed upon the island
of Cyprus for Desdemona to have committed the crime for which
Othello murders her. To maintain the intensity of his play Shakespeare has Othello and Desdemona consummate their wedding
on the first night on Cyprus, thus radically altering Cinthio's

account, in which they had lived happily together in Venice for some time before the Cyprus expedition. It was important for the play that Othello be allowed no time in which to consider Desdemona's conduct carefully or to consult with anyone other than Iago. Othello must move from Iago's first suggestion to the murder of Desdemona without pause of reflection.

Although such rapid passage of time was necessary for his play, Shakespeare did take means of obscuring from the audience the resulting violations of logical probability. He used a device that critics have come to call "double time." The play moves on two time sequences at the same time: during the last four acts, while the action is moving forward at so rapid a pace upon the stage, by passing hints, references, and allusions Shakespeare suggests that larger periods of time are passing and that Othello has had ample time to be concerned about an adultery that has been going on over a long period. Shakespeare maintains at the same time a rapid time scheme to prevent the audience from questioning Othello's belief in Iago, and a slow one to obscure the resulting absurdity of an adultery having taken place under physically impossible conditions in so brief a period. Shakespeare's manipulation of time in *Othello* has been perhaps most perceptively studied by Harley Granville-Barker (*Prefaces to Shakespeare,* Princeton: Princeton University Press, 1947, II, 24–30) who concludes:

> But the overriding explanation of what Shakespeare does here and at similar junctures is that he is not essentially concerned with time and the calendar at all. These, as with the actor and his behaviour, and other outward circumstances, must be given plausibility. But the play's essential action lies in the process of thought and feeling by which the characters are moved and the story is forwarded. And the deeper the springs of these the less do time, place and circumstances affect them. His imagination is now concerned with fundamental passions, and its swift working demands uncumbered expression. He may falsify the calendar for his convenience, but we shall find neither trickery nor anomaly in the fighting of the intellectual battle for Othello's soul. And in the light of the truth of this the rest will pass unnoticed.

THE TRAGEDY OF Othello
THE MOOR OF VENICE

THE NAMES OF THE ACTORS.

DUKE OF VENICE.
BRABANTIO, [*a Senator,*] *father to* DESDEMONA.
SENATORS.
GRATIANO, [*brother to* BRABANTIO,] } *two noble Ve-*
LODOVICO, [*kinsman to* BRABANTIO,] } *netians.*
OTHELLO, *the Moor,* [*in the service of Venice*].
CASSIO, [*his*] *honourable Lieutenant.*
IAGO, [*his Ancient,*] *a villain.*
RODERIGO, *a gull'd* [*Venetian*] *gentleman.*
MONTANO, [*former*] *Governor of Cyprus.*
Clown, [*servant to* OTHELLO].

DESDEMONA, [*daughter to* BRABANTIO *and*] *wife to*
  OTHELLO.
EMILIA, *wife to* IAGO.
BIANCA, *a courtesan,* [*in love with* CASSIO].

Sailor, [*Messenger, Herald, Officers, Gentlemen, Musicians,*
  Attendants].

[SCENE. — *Venice; Cyprus.*]

Act One

◆◆

*Iago – hangs back
in shadows so
he won't be
recognized*

SCENE I. [*Venice. A street.*]

Enter Roderigo *and* Iago.

ROD.   Tush, never tell me! I take it much unkindly
That thou, Iago, who hast had my purse
As if the strings were thine, shouldst know of this.

IAGO. 'Sblood, but you will not hear me!
If ever I did dream of such a matter,   5
Abhor me.

ROD.   Thou told'st me thou didst hold him in thy hate.

IAGO. Despise me if I do not. Three great ones of the city,
In personal suit to make me his lieutenant,
Off-capp'd to him; and, by the faith of man,   10
I know my price, I am worth no worse a place.
But he, as loving his own pride and purposes,
Evades them with a bombast circumstance,
Horribly stuff'd with epithets of war;
And, in conclusion,   15

I.I. This scene takes place at night. It opens in the midst of an excited conversation between Iago and his dupe, the Venetian gallant Roderigo, who is upbraid-
ing him for concealing some matter of great importance. What this is we learn at
the end of the scene [K].   3 *this* the marriage of Othello and Desdemona.   4
'Sblood by God's blood.   6 *Abhor* shrink in horror from.   7 *him* Othello.
9 *In personal suit* requesting in person.   10 *Off-capp'd* stood with hat in hand,
a sign of respect and subservience.   11 *price* value, worth. *worse a place*
lower a position.   13 *bombast circumstance* bombastic circumlocution. "Bombast"
is literally a kind of cotton padding.   14 *epithets* technical terms.

Nonsuits my mediators; for, "Certes," says he,
"I have already chose my officer."
And what was he?
Forsooth, a great arithmetician,
One Michael Cassio, a Florentine   20
(A fellow almost damn'd in a fair wife),
That never set a squadron in the field,
Nor the division of a battle knows
More than a spinster; unless the bookish theoric,
Wherein the toged consuls can propose   25
As masterly as he. Mere prattle, without practice,
Is all his soldiership. But he, sir, had th' election;
And I (of whom his eyes had seen the proof
At Rhodes, at Cyprus, and on other grounds
Christian and heathen) must be belee'd and calm'd   30
By debitor and creditor, this counter-caster.
He (in good time!) must his lieutenant be,
And I (God bless the mark!) his Moorship's ancient.

ROD.   By heaven, I rather would have been his hangman.

IAGO.   Why, there's no remedy; 'tis the curse of service.   35
Preferment goes by letter and affection,
And not by old gradation, where each second
Stood heir to th' first. Now, sir, be judge yourself,

---

16 *Nonsuits my mediators* denies the pleas of those who had interceded for me.
Certes certainly.   19 *arithmetician* Iago has the veteran's contempt for the
scientific soldier who knows more of mathematics than of actual warfare [K].
20 *Florentine* Since the Florentines were great merchants, he may also alude to
Cassio's bookkeeping accomplishments, to which he refers in line 31 [K].   21 *A
fellow . . . wife* A puzzling line which has been much disputed. An Italian proverb
holds that a man with a fair wife is damned. Perhaps he means that Cassio is
about to marry. Perhaps Shakespeare at the time he wrote the line meant to follow Cinthio, in whose account Cassio is married.   23 *division of a battle* how an
army should be drawn up [K].   24 *unless . . . theoric* except in pedantic theory
[K].   25 *toged consuls* the Venetian senators wearing the toga, a traditional robe
of peace. *propose* speak.   27 *had th' election* was chosen.   30 *must be belee'd
and calm'd* must "have the wind taken out of my sails," as we say. A boat is
"belee'd" when another runs between her and the wind so that she is "to the lee-
ward." Thus she is more or less "becalmed" and loses headway. The nautical metaphor is appropriate for a Venetian officer [K].   31 *debitor and creditor* bookkeeper.
counter-caster one who makes petty computations by means of counters—tokens,

Whether I in any just term am affin'd
To love the Moor.

ROD.   I would not follow him then.   40

IAGO.   O, sir, content you.
I follow him to serve my turn upon him.
We cannot all be masters, nor all masters
Cannot be truly follow'd. You shall mark
Many a duteous and knee-crooking knave   45
That, doting on his own obsequious bondage,
Wears out his time, much like his master's ass,
For naught but provender; and when he's old, cashier'd.
Whip me such honest knaves! Others there are
Who, trimm'd in forms and visages of duty,   50
Keep yet their hearts attending on themselves;
And, throwing but shows of service on their lords,
Do well thrive by them, and when they have lin'd their
    coats,
Do themselves homage. These fellows have some soul;
And such a one do I profess myself. For, sir,   55
It is as sure as you are Roderigo,
Were I the Moor, I would not be Iago.
In following him, I follow but myself;
Heaven is my judge, not I for love and duty,
But seeming so, for my peculiar end;   60

---

pieces of metal or uncurrent coin used in "casting" accounts or making change [K].
33 *bless the mark* avert the evil omen (a common expression). *ancient* ensign, literally a standard-bearer.   35 *service* military service.   36–7 *Preferment . . . old
gradation* promotion depends upon influence (letter) and favouritism (affection)
rather than upon the old way of promotion from grade to grade according to
seniority.   39–40 *Whether . . . To love the Moor* whether I stand in any such
relation to the Moor as justly binds me to love him [K].   *term* manner.   *affin'd* re-
lated.   44 *truly* loyally.   45 *knee-crooking* flattering, subservient.   *knave* fellow.
46 *doting on* loving beyond reason.   47 *time* lifetime.   48 *cashier'd* dismissed from
service.   49 *Whip me* let them be whipped (for all I care).   *honest* honourable.
knaves fellows.   50 *trimm'd* dressed, ornamented.   *forms and visages* manners
and outward appearances.   *duty* loyalty.   52 *throwing* bestowing.   *shows* appearances.   53 *lin'd their coats* enriched themselves.   54 *Do themselves homage*
abandon their masters and serve only themselves [K].   57 *Were I . . . be Iago*
This amounts to an assertion that Iago is always himself—always devoted to his
own interests [K]. Each man is what he is, and were he someone else (the Moor) he
would not be what he now is (Iago).   60 *peculiar* special, personal.

For when my outward action doth demonstrate
The native act and figure of my heart
In compliment extern, 'tis not long after
But I will wear my heart upon my sleeve
For daws to peck at. I am not what I am.   65

ROD.   What a full fortune does the thick-lips owe
If he can carry't thus!

IAGO.   Call up her father,
Rouse him. — Make after him, poison his delight,
Proclaim him in the streets. Incense her kinsmen,
And though he in a fertile climate dwell,   70
Plague him with flies; though that his joy be joy,
Yet throw such changes of vexation on't
As it may lose some colour.

ROD.   Here is her father's house. I'll call aloud.

IAGO.   Do, with like timorous accent and dire yell   75
As when, by night and negligence, the fire
Is spied in populous cities.

ROD.   What, ho, Brabantio! Signior Brabantio, ho!

IAGO.   Awake! What, ho, Brabantio! Thieves! thieves! thieves!
Look to your house, your daughter, and your bags!   80
Thieves! thieves!

                    [Enter] Brabantio above, at a window.

BRA.   What is the reason of this terrible summons?
What is the matter there?

ROD.   Signior, is all your family within?

IAGO.   Are your doors lock'd?

BRA.   Why, wherefore ask you this?   85

---

62 native act and figure true actions and feelings.   63 compliment extern outward
appearance and behaviour [K].   65 daws jackdaws, proverbially stupid birds (F¹; Q¹:
"doues").   66 full fortune good luck. owe possess.   67 carry't thus get away with
what he has done.   68 after him Othello.   70 in a fertile climate dwell is enjoy-
ing abundant good fortune [K].   71 flies petty annoyances.   72 changes of vexation vexatious disturbances.   73 As so that. it his joy. lose some colour be
tarnished.   75 like timorous accent such terrifying voice.   80 bags money bags.
86 Zounds by God's wounds. For shame . . . gown Iago means that it is shameful

IAGO.	Zounds, sir, y'are robb'd! For shame put on your gown!
	Your heart is burst; you have lost half your soul.
	<u>Even now, now, very now, an old black ram</u>
	Is tupping your white ewe. Arise, arise!
	Awake the snorting citizens with the bell,
	Or else the devil will make a grandsire of you.
	Arise, I say!

90

| BRA. | What, have you lost your wits? |

| ROD. | Most reverend signior, do you know my voice? |

| BRA. | Not I. What are you? |

| ROD. | My name is Roderigo. |

| BRA. | The worser welcome! |

95

I have charg'd thee not to haunt about my doors.
In honest plainness thou hast heard me say
My daughter is not for thee; and now, in madness,
Being full of supper and distemp'ring draughts,
Upon malicious bravery dost thou come

100

To start my quiet.

| ROD. | Sir, sir, sir — |

| BRA. | But thou must needs be sure |

My spirit and my place have in them power
To make this bitter to thee.

| ROD. | Patience, good sir. |

| BRA. | What tell'st thou me of robbing? This is Venice; |

105

My house is not a grange.

| ROD. | Most grave Brabantio, |

In simple and pure soul I come to you.

---

for Brabantio to be sleeping when he ought to be up and dressed attending to his affairs [K]. *gown* dressing gown.   89 *tupping* covering.   90 *snorting* snoring. *bell* tocsin, general alarm bell.   91 *the devil* traditionally represented as black. 99 *distemp'ring draughts* intoxicating drinks.   100 *Upon malicious bravery* on account of a malicious wish to defy me—to brave my wrath [K].   101 *start* startle, disturb.   *quiet* sleep.   103 *place* position (as senator).   106 *grange* lonely farm-house.   107 *simple* honest, sincere.

IAGO.   Zounds, sir, you are one of those that will not serve God
         if the devil bid you. Because we come to do you service,
         and you think we are ruffians, you'll have your daughter   110
         cover'd with a Barbary horse; you'll have your nephews
         neigh to you; you'll have coursers for cousins, and
         gennets for germans.

BRA.   What profane wretch art thou?

IAGO.   I am one, sir, that come to tell you your daughter and   115
         the Moor are now making the beast with two backs.

BRA.   Thou art a villain.

IAGO.   You are a senator.

BRA.   This thou shalt answer. I know thee, Roderigo.

ROD.   Sir, I will answer anything. But I beseech you,
         If't be your pleasure and most wise consent   120
         (As partly I find it is) that your fair daughter,
         At this odd-even and dull watch o' th' night,
         Transported, with no worse nor better guard
         But with a knave of common hire, a gondolier,
         To the gross clasps of a lascivious Moor —   125
         If this be known to you, and your allowance,
         We then have done you bold and saucy wrongs;
         But if you know not this, my manners tell me
         We have your wrong rebuke. Do not believe
         That, from the sense of all civility,   130
         I thus would play and trifle with your reverence.
         Your daughter, if you have not given her leave,
         I say again, hath made a gross revolt,

108-9 *you are one . . . bid you* You are one of those men that will not take the
best advice in the world if it comes from a person that you do not like [K].   111
nephews grandsons.   113 *gennets for germans* horses (of a Spanish breed) for
kinsmen.   114 *profane* foul-mouthed [K].   118 *answer* be called to account for.
122 *odd-even* about midnight, when one hardly knows whether it is night or morning [K].   *dull watch* sleepy time of night.   126 *your allowance* approved by you.
127 *saucy* insolent.   128 *manners* knowledge of proper behaviour—of the way
gentlemen should treat each other [K].   130 *from . . . civility* contrary to proper
and decent behaviour.   131 *your reverence* the respect to which you are entitled.
133 *gross* indecent   135 *extravagant* wandering. *wheeling* having no fixed abode

Tying her duty, beauty, wit, and fortunes
In an extravagant and wheeling stranger   135
Of here and everywhere. Straight satisfy yourself.
If she be in her chamber, or your house,
Let loose on me the justice of the state
For thus deluding you.

BRA.   Strike on the tinder, ho!
Give me a taper! Call up all my people!   140
This accident is not unlike my dream.
Belief of it oppresses me already.
Light, I say! light!   *Exit [above].*

IAGO.   Farewell, for I must leave you.
It seems not meet, nor wholesome to my place,
To be produc'd (as, if I stay, I shall)   145
Against the Moor. For I do know the state,
However this may gall him with some check,
Cannot with safety cast him; for he's embark'd
With such loud reason to the Cyprus wars,
Which even now stand in act, that for their souls   150
Another of his fathom they have none
To lead their business; in which regard,
Though I do hate him as I do hell pains,
Yet, for necessity of present life,
I must show out a flag and sign of love,   155
Which is indeed but sign. That you shall surely find him,
Lead to the Sagittary the raised search;
And there will I be with him. So farewell.   *Exit.*

        Enter, [below,] Brabantio, in his night-
        gown, and Servants with torches.

[K]. *stranger* alien.   136 *Straight* immediately.   *satisfy* inform.   140 *taper* candle.
141 *accident* event.   *dream* To be taken literally rather than in the sense of "what
I thought might happen"; for Brabantio has had no suspicion of Desdemona's love
for Othello. We are to suppose he had had a bad dream, which he now thinks was
prophetic [K].   144 *meet* proper.   *wholesome* healthy.   *to my place* for my position (as Othello's ensign).   145 *produc'd* made a witness.   147 *gall* annoy.   *check*
reprimand.   148 *cast* dismiss.   149 *loud* urgent.   150 *stand in act* are in progress.
151 *fathom* capacity, ability.   154 *life* livelihood.   156 *That* so that.   157 *Sagittary* probably the name of an inn with an archer or centaur with drawn bow on
its signboard.

BRA.   It is too true an evil. Gone she is;
        And what's to come of my despised time   160
        Is naught but bitterness. Now, Roderigo,
        Where didst thou see her? — O unhappy girl! —
        With the Moor, say'st thou? — Who would be a father? —
        How didst thou know 'twas she? — O, she deceives me
        Past thought! — What said she to you? — Get moe tapers!   165
        Raise all my kindred! — Are they married, think you?

ROD.   Truly I think they are.

BRA.   O heaven! How got she out? O treason of the blood!
        Fathers, from hence trust not your daughters' minds
        By what you see them act. Is there not charms   170
        By which the property of youth and maidhood
        May be abus'd? Have you not read, Roderigo,
        Of some such thing?

ROD.   Yes, sir, I have indeed.

BRA.   Call up my brother. — O, would you had had her! —
        Some one way, some another. — Do you know   175
        Where we may apprehend her and the Moor?

ROD.   I think I can discover him, if you please
        To get good guard and go along with me.

BRA.   Pray you lead on. At every house I'll call;
        I may command at most. — Get weapons, ho!   180
        And raise some special officers of night. —
        On, good Roderigo. I'll deserve your pains.   *Exeunt.*

---

160 *what's . . . time* the remainder of my life.   165 *moe* more.   168 *treason of
the blood* treachery of my own child.   170 *charms* magic spells.   171 *property*
special quality.   172 *abus'd* deceived, deluded, led astray. Belief in love charms
(philtres) was prevalent in Shakespeare's time. See Kitttredge, WITCHCRAFT IN OLD
AND NEW ENGLAND, Chapter IV [K].   177 *discover* uncover.   180 *I may command
at most* at most of the houses. Brabantio is a person of such high rank and such
extensive family connections that he can summon the retainers of almost any
house to his aid [K].   181 *raise . . . night* call to my assistance some of the
officers whose special duty it is to guard the city by night [K].   182 *deserve your
pains* show myself grateful for the exertion you make in my behalf.

I.II. 2 *very . . . conscience* a matter of strict conscientious scruple; something
that conscience imperatively requires [K].   3 *contriv'd* deliberate.   5 *yerk'd*

◇◇◇◇◇◇◇◇◇◇◇◇◇◇◇◇

SCENE II. [*Venice. Another street.*]

Enter Othello, Iago, *and* Attendants *with torches.*

IAGO.   Though in the trade of war I have slain men,
      Yet do I hold it very stuff o' th' conscience
      To do no contriv'd murder. I lack iniquity
      Sometimes to do me service. Nine or ten times
      I had thought t' have yerk'd him here under the ribs.   5

OTH.   'Tis better as it is.

IAGO.   Nay, but he prated,
      And spoke such scurvy and provoking terms
      Against your honour
      That with the little godliness I have
      I did full hard forbear him. But I pray you, sir,   10
      Are you fast married? Be assur'd of this,
      That the magnifico is much belov'd,
      And hath in his effect a voice potential —
      As double as the Duke's. He will divorce **you**,
      Or put upon you what restraint and grievance   15
      The law, with all his might to enforce it **on**,
      Will give him cable.

OTH.   Let him do his spite.
      My services which I have done the signiory
      Shall outtongue his complaints. 'Tis yet to know —

---

jabbed.   *him* Roderigo, whose coversation Iago is now reporting to Othello.
7 *scurvy* insulting.   **10** *did full . . . him* with difficulty kept my hands off him.
12 *magnifico* Venetian lord, Brabantio.   **13** *in his . . . potential* a powerful voice
when it comes to executing his wishes.   **14** *double as the Duke's* The Doge (Duke
of Venice) was commonly, though erroneously, believed by the Elizabethans to
have two votes. Hence Iago says, hyperbolically, that Brabantio's voice (or vote) is
as much a double vote as the Duke's itself [K].   **16** *enforce it on* force it (the law)
to be executed with utmost rigour.   **17** *cable* scope (another nautical metaphor).
17 *do his spite* do the utmost that his enmity can accomplish [K].   **18** *signiory*
governing body of Venice.   **19** *outtongue* speak louder than.

Which, when I know that boasting is an honour,   20
I shall promulgate — I fetch my life and being
From men of royal siege; and my demerits
May speak unbonneted to as proud a fortune
As this that I have reach'd. For know, Iago,
But that I love the gentle Desdemona,   25
I would not my unhoused free condition
Put into circumscription and confine
For the sea's worth.

                     Enter Cassio, *and* Officers *with torches.*

                     But look what lights come yond.

IAGO.   Those are the raised father and his friends.
You were best go in.

OTH.   Not I. I must be found.   30
My parts, my title, and my perfect soul
Shall manifest me rightly. Is it they?

IAGO.   By Janus, I think no.

OTH.   The servants of the Duke? and my lieutenant?
The goodness of the night upon you, friends!   35
What is the news?

CAS.   The Duke does greet you, General;
And he requires your haste-post-haste appearance
Even on the instant.

OTH.   What's the matter, think you?

CAS.   Something from Cyprus, as I may divine.

20–1 *Which, when* . . . *promulgate* The inference is that Othello does not intend
to disclose his royal descent until he finds that honour demands that he make it
public [K]. 22 *siege* literally seat, hence rank. *demerits* deserts. 23 *May speak*
. . . . *fortune* entitle me to meet unabashed even so great an honour as an alliance
with Brabantio's family—I say it with all due modesty [K]. *unbonneted* courte-
ously, hat in hand—not arrogantly, as with his hat on his head [K]. It is more
likely, from the context of the term, that it means the opposite: that Othello
may speak without removing his hat, thus on equal terms. The term has been
much disputed. 26 *unhoused* unconfined, unmarried. 28 *sea's worth* The sea
was regarded as a treasure-house because of the sunken ships on its bottom.

It is a business of some heat. The galleys   40
Have sent a dozen sequent messengers
This very night at one another's heels;
And many of the consuls, rais'd and met,
Are at the Duke's already. You have been hotly call'd for;
When, being not at your lodging to be found,   45
The Senate hath sent about three several quests
To search you out.

OTH.   'Tis well I am found by you.
I will but spend a word here in the house,
And go with you.   *[Exit.]*

CAS.   Ancient, what makes he here?

IAGO.   Faith, he to-night hath boarded a land carack.   50
If it prove lawful prize, he's made for ever.

CAS.   I do not understand.

IAGO.   He's married.

CAS.   To who?

                    [Enter Othello.]

IAGO.   Marry, to — Come, Captain, will you go?

OTH.   Have with you.

CAS.   Here comes another troop to seek for you.

                    Enter Brabantio, Roderigo, *and* Officers
                    with torches and weapons.

IAGO.   It is Brabantio. General, be advis'd.   55
He comes to bad intent.

---

29 *raised* roused to action—not roused from sleep [ĸ].   31-2 *My parts . . . me*
rightly my past deeds (which have all been honourable), my title as general-in-
chief (which vouches for my honour), and finally, my unblemished conscience will
surely do me justice—justify me [ĸ].   33 *Janus* a two-faced god.   41 *sequent* one
after another.   50 *carack* merchant vessel.   52 *To who* Cassio either does not
know of the elopement or does not choose to disclose his knowledge to Iago. Cassio
had often been a messenger in the course of Othello's wooing (III.III.94–100, 111–
12), but nothing in the play indicates that he was now aware of the marriage [ĸ].
55 *advis'd* cautious.

OTH.   Holla! stand there!

ROD.   Signior, it is the Moor.

BRA.   Down with him, thief!

[*They draw on both sides.*]

IAGO.   You, Roderigo! Come, sir, I am for you.

OTH.   Keep up your bright swords, for the dew will rust them.
          Good signior, you shall more command with years   60
          Than with your weapons.

BRA.   O thou foul thief, where hast thou stow'd my daughter?
          Damn'd as thou art, thou hast enchanted her!
          For I'll refer me to all things of sense,
          If she in chains of magic were not bound,   65
          Whether a maid so tender, fair, and happy,
          So opposite to marriage that she shunn'd
          The wealthy curled darlings of our nation,
          Would ever have (t' incur a general mock)
          Run from her guardage to the sooty bosom   70
          Of such a thing as thou — to fear, not to delight.
          Judge me the world if 'tis not gross in sense
          That thou hast practis'd on her with foul charms,
          Abus'd her delicate youth with drugs or minerals
          That weaken motion. I'll have't disputed on.   75
          'Tis probable, and palpable to thinking.
          I therefore apprehend and do attach thee
          For an abuser of the world, a practiser
          Of arts inhibited and out of warrant.

---

58 *You, Roderigo . . . you* Probably Iago wishes to protect Roderigo so that he can
continue to supply him with money. His singling out a weak opponent is not to
be taken as a sign of cowardice in Iago.   59 *bright swords* A trace of the soldier's
contempt for armed civilians [K]. Othello speaks with the calm self-assurance of
the professional soldier.   62 *stow'd* bestowed, hidden.   64 *refer me . . . sense*
appeal for judgment to all creatures that have their senses [K].   67 *opposite to
marriage* This indicates merely that Desdemona had never favoured any of the
Venetian gallants who had wooed her, not that she was more averse to marriage
than other girls her age [K].   69 *general mock* universal ridicule.   70 *her
guardage* my guardianship.   72 *Judge me the world* let the whole world judge
for me [K].   *gross in sense* obvious (large) to ordinary perception.   73 *practis'd*
acted with evil intent, imposed.   74 *Abus'd . . . youth* deluded her, young and
delicate as she is, and therefore easily influenced by magic [K].   75 *That weaken*

Lay hold upon him. If he do resist,   80
Subdue him at his peril.

OTH.   Hold your hands,
Both you of my inclining and the rest.
Were it my cue to fight, I should have known it
Without a prompter. Where will you that I go
To answer this your charge?

BRA.   To prison, till fit time   85
Of law and course of direct session
Call thee to answer.

OTH.   What if I do obey?
How may the Duke be therewith satisfied,
Whose messengers are here about my side
Upon some present business of the state   90
To bring me to him?

OFFICER.   'Tis true, most worthy signior.
The Duke's in council, and your noble self
I am sure is sent for.

BRA.   How? The Duke in council?
In this time of the night? Bring him away!
Mine's not an idle cause. The Duke himself,   95
Or any of my brothers of the state,
Cannot but feel this wrong as 'twere their own;
For if such actions may have passage free,
Bondslaves and pagans shall our statesmen be.

                                          Exeunt.

---

motion that dull the perceptive faculties. The point is that unless her mind and
perceptions had been disordered she would have seen Othello as he was—ugly, and
not attractive [K]. *motion* normal reaction. *disputed on* debated (by experts).
79 *inhibited* prohibited. *out of warrant* illegal.   82 *of my inclining* who are
ready to take sides with me [K].   85–6 *fit time . . . law* the time legally appointed
in the court calendar for a regular session of the court. Brabantio means that
Othello shall be confined until the next court sits [K].   90 *present* immediate,
urgent.   99 *Bondslaves . . . be* slaves and pagans will be at liberty to marry
our daughters and their descendants will rule the Venetian state. Brabantio meets
the difficulty raised by Othello with respect to the Duke's mandate by insisting
that the case may be heard at once by the Duke and Senators, since they are
already in session [K].

◇◇◇◇◇◇◇◇◇◇◇◇◇◇◇

SCENE III. [*Venice. A council chamber.*]

Enter Duke *and* Senators, *set at a table, with lights and*
Attendants.

DUKE.   There is no composition in these news
That gives them credit.

1. SEN.   Indeed they are disproportion'd.
My letters say a hundred and seven galleys.

DUKE.   And mine a hundred forty.

2. SEN.   And mine two hundred.
But though they jump not on a just account   5
(As in these cases where the aim reports
'Tis oft with difference), yet do they all confirm
A Turkish fleet, and bearing up to Cyprus.

DUKE.   Nay, it is possible enough to judgment.
I do not so secure me in the error   10
But the main article I do approve
In fearful sense.

SAILOR.   (*within*) What, ho! what, ho! what, ho!

                        Enter Sailor.

OFFICER.   A messenger from the galleys.

DUKE.   Now, what's the business?

SAILOR.   The Turkish preparation makes for Rhodes.
So was I bid report here to the state   15
By Signior Angelo.

I.III. 1 *composition* consistency.   2 *credit* credibility. *disproportion'd* inconsistent.
5 *jump not* disagree.   *just account* accurate number.   6–7 *As in . . . difference*
as in cases like this, where reports are made on the basis of guesswork, there is
often a discrepancy [K].   10–12 *I do not so . . . sense* I do not allow the incon-
sistency in numbers to make me feel so free from anxiety as to prevent me from
crediting the main point of the dispatches—and that too, in a way that makes me
anxious [K].   11 *article* item.   *approve* believe.   16 *Signior Angelo* probably the
commander of the galleys.   18 *assay of reason* test which reason can apply.   *pageant* mere spectacle or show.   19 *false gaze* looking in the wrong direction.
23 *may* can.   *more facile question* less arduous fighting. To "question" is to "con-

DUKE.   How say you by this change?

1. SEN.   This cannot be
By no assay of reason. 'Tis a pageant
To keep us in false gaze. When we consider
Th' importancy of Cyprus to the Turk,   20
And let ourselves again but understand
That, as it more concerns the Turk than Rhodes,
So may he with more facile question bear it,
For that it stands not in such warlike brace,
But altogether lacks th' abilities   25
That Rhodes is dress'd in — if we make thought of this,
We must not think the Turk is so unskilful
To leave that latest which concerns him first,
Neglecting an attempt of ease and gain
To wake and wage a danger profitless.   30

DUKE.   Nay, in all confidence he's not for Rhodes.

OFFICER. Here is more news.

                    Enter a Messenger.

MESS.   The Ottomites, reverend and gracious,
Steering with due course toward the isle of Rhodes,
Have there injointed them with an after fleet.   35

1. SEN. Ay, so I thought. How many, as you guess?

MESS.   Of thirty sail; and now they do restem
Their backward course, bearing with frank appearance
Their purposes toward Cyprus. Signior Montano,
Your trusty and most valiant servitor,   40
With his free duty recommends you thus,

---

test." *bear it* capture it.   24 *For that* because. *in such warlike brace* so well
prepared to withstand an attack. The figure is of a person who is "braced" (in a
posture of defence) to meet a blow or an assault [K].   25 *abilities* means of defence.   26 *dress'd in* equipped with.   27 *unskilful* undiscriminating, lacking in
judgment [K].   29 *attempt* undertaking. *of ease and gain* easy and profitable.
30 *wake* stir up. *wage* risk.   35 *injointed them* joined themselves. *after* second.
37–8 *restem . . . course* steer their course back again [K].   38 *frank appearance*
no attempt at concealment.   41 *free duty* expressions of unqualified respect.
recommends informs, reports to.

And prays you to believe him.

DUKE. 'Tis certain then for Cyprus.
Marcus Luccicos, is not he in town?

1. SEN. He's now in Florence. 45

DUKE. Write from us to him; post-post-haste dispatch.

Enter Brabantio, Othello, Cassio, Iago,
Roderigo, *and* Officers.

1. SEN. Here comes Brabantio and the valiant Moor.

DUKE. Valiant Othello, we must straight employ you
Against the general enemy Ottoman.
[*To* Brabantio] I did not see you. Welcome, gentle
signior. 50
We lack'd your counsel and your help to-night.

BRA. So did I yours. Good your Grace, pardon me.
Neither my place, nor aught I heard **of** business,
Hath rais'd me from my bed; nor doth the general care
Take hold on me; for my particular grief 55
Is of so floodgate and o'erbearing nature
That it engluts and swallows other sorrows,
And it is still itself.

DUKE. Why, what's the matter?

BRA. My daughter! O, my daughter!

ALL. Dead?

BRA. Ay, to me!
She is abus'd, stol'n from me, and corrupted 60

---

44 *Marcus Luccicos* A strange name, which may or may not be misprinted. Doubtless some foreigner in the service of the Venetian state [K]. 48 *straight* at once.
49 *general enemy* the enemy of all Christendom [K]. 55 *particular* personal.
56 *floodgate* like a sluice-gate, which when opened allowed the water (his tears) to
pour through. *o'erbearing* overwhelming. 57 *engluts* swallows. 58 *And . . .
itself* it remains distinct and unchanged after it has swallowed up all other sorrows
[K]. 60 *abus'd* deluded. 61 *bought of mountebanks* Brabantio's belief that
Othello has used love charms hås become so definite that he 'actually adds a detail
with regard to the persons from whom Othello procured them. Mountebanks
(strolling quacks) were well known to deal in such wares [K]. 62 *prepost'rously*
absurdly. *err* go wrong, become abnormal. 63 *deficient* feeble-minded. *lame
of sense* crippled in mental power. 64 *Sans* without. 66 *beguil'd . . . herself*

By spells and medicines bought of mountebanks;
For nature so prepost'rously to err,
Being not deficient, blind, or lame of sense,
Sans witchcraft could not.

DUKE.   Whoe'er he be that in this foul proceeding   65
Hath thus beguil'd your daughter of herself,
And you of her, the bloody book of law
You shall yourself read in the bitter letter
After your own sense; yea, though our proper son
Stood in your action.

BRA.   Humbly I thank your Grace.   70
Here is the man — this Moor, whom now, it seems,
Your special mandate, for the state affairs,
Hath hither brought.

ALL.   We are very sorry for't.

DUKE.   [*to* Othello] What, in your own part, can you say to this?

BRA.   Nothing, but this is so.   75

OTH.   Most potent, grave, and reverend signiors,
My very noble, and approv'd good masters,
That I have ta'en away this old man's daughter,
It is most true; true I have married her.
The very head and front of my offending   80
Hath this extent, no more. Rude am I in my speech,
And little bless'd with the soft phrase of peace;
For since these arms of mine had seven years' pith
Till now some nine moons wasted, they have us'd
Their dearest action in the tented field;   85

---

cheated your daughter of herself; by means of charms caused her to be something
other than she normally is.   67 *bloody book of law* The punishment for witchcraft was death, practically everywhere in the world [K].   69 *After your own
sense* according to whatever interpretation you may choose to put upon it—i.e.
upon the letter of the law. The passage is not to be taken with strict literalness.
The Duke means that Brabantio shall have the satisfaction of seeing the law executed with all the rigour that he could possibly wish [K].   69 *proper* own.
70 *Stood* were the defendant.   *action* lawsuit.   80 *head and front* entire substance.
81 *Rude* unpolished, unpractised in the art of the orator [K].   82 *soft phrase of
peace* mild and insinuating eloquence that befits an advocate or politician [K].
83 *pith* strength.   84 *moons wasted* months ago.   85 *dearest* most intense.

And little of this great world can I speak
More than pertains to feats of broil and battle;
And therefore little shall I grace my cause
In speaking for myself. Yet, by your gracious patience,
I will a round unvarnish'd tale deliver   90
Of my whole course of love — what drugs, what charms,
What conjuration, and what mighty magic
(For such proceeding am I charg'd withal)
I won his daughter.

BRA.   A maiden never bold;
Of spirit so still and quiet that her motion   95
Blush'd at herself; and she — in spite of nature,
Of years, of country, credit, everything —
To fall in love with what she fear'd to look on!
It is a judgment maim'd and most imperfect
That will confess perfection so could err   100
Against all rules of nature, and must be driven
To find out practices of cunning hell
Why this should be. I therefore vouch again
That with some mixtures pow'rful o'er the blood,
Or with some dram, conjur'd to this effect,   105
He wrought upon her.

DUKE.   To vouch this is no proof,
Without more certain and more overt test
Than these thin habits and poor likelihoods
Of modern seeming do prefer against him.

1. SEN. But, Othello, speak.   110
Did you by indirect and forced courses
Subdue and poison this young maid's affections?
Or came it by request, and such fair question
As soul to soul affordeth?

---

88 *grace my cause* make my case attractive (by eloquent language).   90 *round*
plain.   95-6 *her motion . . . herself* any strong emotion made her blush at herself as if it were an indecorum [K].   *motion* emotion.   97 *credit* reputation.
100 *confess* believe.   101 *driven* obliged, forced.   102 *find out* discover.   *practices*
evil devices, machinations.   103 *vouch* assert.   104 *blood* passions.   105 *conjur'd*
made effective by means of spells.   107 *overt test* tangible evidence.   108 *thin
habits* flimsy coverings (habits) of slight evidence.   *poor likelihoods* mere conjec-

OTH.   I do beseech you,
        Send for the lady to the Sagittary   115
        And let her speak of me before her father.
        If you do find me foul in her report,
        The trust, the office, I do hold of you
        Not only take away, but let your sentence
        Even fall upon my life.

DUKE.   Fetch Desdemona hither.   120

OTH.   Ancient, conduct them; you best know the place.

                Exeunt [Iago *and*] *two or three* [At-
                tendants].

        And till she come, as truly as to heaven
        I do confess the vices of my blood,
        So justly to your grave ears I'll present
        How I did thrive in this fair lady's love,   125
        And she in mine.

DUKE.   Say it, Othello.

OTH.   Her father lov'd me, oft invited me;
        Still question'd me the story of my life
        From year to year — the battles, sieges, fortunes   130
        That I have pass'd.
        I ran it through, even from my boyish days
        To th' very moment that he bade me tell it.
        Wherein I spake of most disastrous chances,
        Of moving accidents by flood and field;   135
        Of hairbreadth scapes i' th' imminent deadly breach;
        Of being taken by the insolent foe
        And sold to slavery; of my redemption thence
        And portance in my travel's history;

---

tures.   109 *modern* commonplace.   111 *indirect* underhanded. *forced courses*
violent means.   113-14 *such fair . . . affordeth* such fair words as a lover uses
when he speaks heart-to-heart with his ladylove [K].   117 *foul* guilty.   123 *vices
of my blood* faults of my nature [K].   129 *Still* continually.   135 *moving accidents* affecting or stirring events — such adventures as would thrill the hearer [K].
136 *th' imminent deadly breach* the breach (in the wall of a city or fortress) which
threatened death [K].   139 *portance* bearing, conduct.

Wherein of antres vast and deserts idle,   140
Rough quarries, rocks, and hills whose heads touch
      heaven,
It was my hint to speak — such was the process;
And of the Cannibals that each other eat,
The Anthropophagi, and men whose heads
Do grow beneath their shoulders. This to hear   145
Would Desdemona seriously incline;
But still the house affairs would draw her thence;
Which ever as she could with haste dispatch,
She'ld come again, and with a greedy ear
Devour up my discourse. Which I observing,   150
Took once a pliant hour, and found good means
To draw from her a prayer of earnest heart
That I would all my pilgrimage dilate,
Whereof by parcels she had something heard,
But not intentively. I did consent,   155
And often did beguile her of her tears
When I did speak of some distressful stroke
That my youth suffer'd. My story being done,
She gave me for my pains a world of sighs.
She swore, in faith, 'twas strange, 'twas passing strange;   160
'Twas pitiful, 'twas wondrous pitiful.
She wish'd she had not heard it; yet she wish'd
That heaven had made her such a man. She thank'd me;
And bade me, if I had a friend that lov'd her,
I should but teach him how to tell my story,   165
And that would woo her. Upon this hint I spake.
She lov'd me for the dangers I had pass'd,

---

140 *antres* caves. *idle* empty, desolate.   142 *hint* occasion.   144 *Anthropophagi*
man-eaters. Shakespeare here is drawing upon the travel literature widely popular
in his day.   144-5 *heads . . . shoulders* Such headless men are specifically men-
tioned in Pliny's NATURAL HISTORY and in Sir Walter Raleigh's DISCOVERY OF GUIANA.
147 *still* ever and anon.   151 *pliant hour* a time when I could influence Desdemona and get her to ask, as a favour, what I was myself eager to do [K].   153 *dilate*
narrate fully (not extend).   154 *parcels* small portions.   155 *intentively* in such
a way that she could give her full attention to it [K].   160 *passing* surpassingly.
163 *That heaven . . . a man* There are two interpretations in the field: (a) "that
heaven had created such a man for her" (to be her husband); (b) "that she had
been born a man like me, so that she might have had such adventures and done

And I lov'd her that she did pity them.
This only is the witchcraft I have us'd.
Here comes the lady. Let her witness it.   170

Enter Desdemona, Iago, Attendants.

DUKE. I think this tale would win my daughter too.
Good Brabantio,
Take up this mangled matter at the best.
Men do their broken weapons rather use
Than their bare hands.

BRA.   I pray you hear her speak.   175
If she confess that she was half the wooer,
Destruction on my head if my bad blame
Light on the man! Come hither, gentle mistress.
Do you perceive in all this noble company
Where most you owe obedience?

DES.   My noble father,   180
I do perceive here a divided duty.
To you I am bound for life and education;
My life and education both do learn me
How to respect you: you are the lord of duty;
I am hitherto your daughter. But here's my husband;   185
And so much duty as my mother show'd
To you, preferring you before her father,
So much I challenge that I may profess
Due to the Moor my lord.

BRA.   God b' wi' ye! I have done.
Please it your Grace, on to the state affairs.   190
I had rather to adopt a child than get it.

such deeds." One cannot hesitate long in preferring the second [K].   166 *Upon
this hint* taking advantage of this opportunity [K].   173 *Take up . . . best* make
the best of this confused and confusing business [K].   177 *bad* since in that case
I should do wrong to blame him [K].   182 *education* bringing up.   183 *learn*
teach.   184 *How to respect you* in what light to regard you.   187 *preferring
. . . father* advancing you to a higher position than her father with respect to
duty [K].   188 *challenge . . . profess* claim the right to affirm.   191 *get* beget.
Brabantio thinks that an adopted child would be quite as likely to be dutiful, and
that, if it were not, the father's sorrow would be less than in the case of a child
of his own [K].

Come hither, Moor.
I here do give thee that with all my heart
Which, but thou hast already, with all my heart
I would keep from thee. For your sake, jewel,   195
I am glad at soul I have no other child;
For thy escape would teach me tyranny,
To hang clogs on them. I have done, my lord.

DUKE.   Let me speak like yourself and lay a sentence
Which, as a grise or step, may help these lovers   200
Into your favour.
When remedies are past, the griefs are ended
By seeing the worst, which late on hopes depended.
To mourn a mischief that is past and gone
Is the next way to draw new mischief on.   205
What cannot be preserv'd when fortune takes,
Patience her injury a mock'ry makes.
The robb'd that smiles steals something from the thief;
He robs himself that spends a bootless grief.

BRA.   So let the Turk of Cyprus us beguile: 210
We lose it not, so long as we can smile.
He bears the sentence well that nothing bears
But the free comfort which from thence he hears;
But he bears both the sentence and the sorrow
That to pay grief must of poor patience borrow.   215
These sentences, to sugar, or to gall,
Being strong on both sides, are equivocal.
But words are words. I never yet did hear
That the bruis'd heart was pieced through the ear.

195 *For your sake* on your account.   198 *clogs* shackles.   199 *like yourself* as
you would speak if you were not angry [K].   *lay a sentence* state a principle or
maxim.   200 *grise* step.   202-3 *When remedies . . . depended* one now knows
the worst, whereas a little while ago one's idea of what the worst might be depended on one's fears [K].   *hopes* expectations, fears.   204 *mischief* misfortune.
205 *next* nearest.   206-7 *What cannot . . . makes* when Fortune takes away something that we cannot keep, we make a mockery of her injury by bearing it calmly.
Fortune was conceived more personally by the Elizabethans than by us. She is here
regarded as malicious; and her malice is thwarted when the victim refuses to give
her the satisfaction of seeing that he is distressed [K].   209 *spends a bootless grief*
indulges in unavailing sorrow [K].   216-17 *These sentences . . . equivocal* maxims
such as these are ambiguous, since they have a strong tendency in two directions—

Beseech you, now to the affairs of state.   220

DUKE.   The Turk with a most mighty preparation makes for
Cyprus. Othello, the fortitude of the place is best known
to you; and though we have there a substitute of most
allowed sufficiency, yet opinion, a sovereign mistress of
effects, throws a more safer voice on you. You must   225
therefore be content to slubber the gloss of your new
fortunes with this more stubborn and boist'rous expedition.

OTH.   The tyrant custom, most grave senators,
Hath made the flinty and steel couch of war   230
My thrice-driven bed of down. I do agnize
A natural and prompt alacrity
I find in hardness; and do undertake
These present wars against the Ottomites.
Most humbly, therefore, bending to your state,   235
I crave fit disposition for my wife;
Due reference of place, and exhibition,
With such accommodation and besort
As levels with her breeding.

DUKE.   If you please,
Be't at her father's.

BRA.   I'll not have it so.   240

OTH.   Nor I.

DES.   Nor I. I would not there reside,
To put my father in impatient thoughts

---

to sweeten misfortune and to embitter it [K].   219 *pieced* cured, made of one piece
after being broken.   222 *fortitude* strength.   224 *allowed sufficiency* proven
ability.   224–5 *opinion . . . on you* public opinion, which is important in de-
termining policy, considers you safer to have in the position.   226 *slubber* smear,
tarnish.   227 *boist'rous* rough.   231 *thrice-driven* thrice sorted and winnowed
in order that only the softest feathers might be used [K].   231–3 *agnize . . . hardness* I recognize in my own nature an instinctive and spontaneous stimulus that
I find in hardship [K].   234 *These* MALONE; F¹, Q¹: "This."   235 *state* authority.
236 *fit disposition* proper arrangements.   237 *Due reference of place* a suitable
residence.   *exhibition* monetary allowance.   238 *besort* company, attendants.
239 *levels with* is appropriate to.   *breeding* birth, social position.

By being in his eye. Most gracious Duke,
To my unfolding lend your prosperous ear,
And let me find a charter in your voice,   245
T' assist my simpleness.

DUKE.   What would you, Desdemona?

DES.   That I did love the Moor to live with him,
My downright violence, and storm of fortunes,
May trumpet to the world. My heart's subdu'd   250
Even to the very quality of my lord.
I saw Othello's visage in his mind,
And to his honours and his valiant parts
Did I my soul and fortunes consecrate.
So that, dear lords, if I be left behind,   255
A moth of peace, and he go to the war,
The rights for which I love him are bereft me,
And I a heavy interim shall support
By his dear absence. Let me go with him.

OTH.   Let her have your voices.   260
Vouch with me heaven, I therefore beg it not
To please the palate of my appetite,
Nor to comply with heat — the young affects
In me defunct — and proper satisfaction;
But to be free and bounteous to her mind.   265
And heaven defend your good souls that you think
I will your serious and great business scant —
For she is with me. No, when light-wing'd toys

244 *unfolding* disclosure. *prosperous ear* favourable hearing.   245 *charter in your voice* authority (or encouragement) in your assent [K].   246 *simpleness* lack of skill in pleading.   249 *downright* plain and obvious. *violence* violent action. *storm of fortunes* Desdemona has, as it were, "taken her fortunes (her lot in life) by storm," instead of submitting passively to whatever arrangements for her marriage her father might make [K].   250 *trumpet* proclaim loudly.   250-1 *heart's subdu'd . . . my lord* heart is brought into harmony with the very profession of my husband. I have fallen in love with his profession as well as himself [K].   253 *valiant parts* heroic deeds (in battle).   256 *moth* parasitic idler.   257 *bereft* taken from.   258-9 *And I . . . absence* and besides, I shall have to endure a sad interval of loneliness because of the absence of him who is so dear to me. Thus Desdemona drops her exalted tone and expresses the simple and natural feelings of a wife who misses her husband [K].   260 *voices* votes of approval.   263 *comply with heat* satisfy sexual desire. *young affects* youthful passions.   264 *me* UPTON;

Of feather'd Cupid seel with wanton dullness
My speculative and offic'd instruments,   270
That my disports corrupt and taint my business,
Let housewives make a skillet of my helm,
And all indign and base adversities
Make head against my estimation!

DUKE.   Be it as you shall privately determine,   275
Either for her stay or going. Th' affair cries haste,
And speed must answer it. You must hence to-night.

DES.   To-night, my lord?

DUKE.   This night.

OTH.   With all my heart.

DUKE.   At nine i' th' morning here we'll meet again.
Othello, leave some officer behind,   280
And he shall our commission bring to you;
With such things else of quality and respect
As doth import you.

OTH.   So please your Grace, my ancient.
A man he is of honesty and trust.
To his conveyance I assign my wife,   285
With what else needful your good Grace shall think
To be sent after me.

DUKE.   Let it be so.

F¹,Q¹: "my."   264 *defunct* Othello means, not that passion is dead in him, but simply that the ungovernable force of youthful passion is held in check by the self-control of mature years [K]. Yet Shakespeare is anxious to stress that the relation
between Desdemona and Othello is one in which sexual passion is not important.
proper satisfaction my own self-gratification [K].   265 *mind* wishes.   268 *For* because. *light-wing'd* frivolous. *toys* trifles.   269 *seel* sew up.   270 *speculative* . . .
instruments my organs of sight (the eyes of my mind), which have their imperative
duties to perform [K]. The metaphor is from the practice of "seeling," sewing up
the eyes of a hawk with silk in the process of taming it. *offic'd* provided with
duties.   271 *disports* recreations.   *taint* impair.   273-4 *all indign . . . estimation* let all manner of disgraceful calamities gather in a troop to attack my reputation [K].   282 *of quality and respect* pertaining to the honour that is to be yours
and to your high position [K].   283 *import* concern.   285 *conveyance* escort.

Good night to every one. [*To* Brabantio] And, noble
 signior,
If virtue no delighted beauty lack,
Your son-in-law is far more fair than black.   290

1. SEN. Adieu, brave Moor. Use Desdemona well.

BRA. Look to her, Moor, if thou hast eyes to see.
She has deceiv'd her father, and may thee.

Exeunt [Duke, Senators, Officers, &c.].

OTH. My life upon her faith! — Honest Iago,
My Desdemona must I leave to thee.   295
I prithee let thy wife attend on her,
And bring them after in the best advantage.
Come, Desdemona. I have but an hour
Of love, of worldly matters and direction,
To spend with thee. We must obey the time. 300

Exeunt Moor *and* Desdemona.

[margin handwritten: Othello's trust in Iago.]

ROD. Iago.

IAGO. What say'st thou, noble heart?

ROD. What will I do, think'st thou?

IAGO. Why, go to bed and sleep.

ROD. I will incontinently drown myself.   305

IAGO. If thou dost, I shall never love thee after. Why, thou
silly gentleman!

ROD. It is silliness to live when to live is torment; and then
have we a prescription to die when death is our physician.

IAGO. O villainous! I have look'd upon the world for four times 310

289 *delighted* endowed with delight (an adjective). 297 *in the best advantage*
as soon as you have a favourable opportunity [K]. 300 *the time* the necessity of
the moment. 305 *incontinently* immediately. 309 *prescription* a prescriptive
right—with a bitter pun on the medical meaning [K]. 316 *fond* foolishly in love.
321 *hyssop* an herb of the mint family. *thyme* another aromatic herb. *gender*
kind, species. 322 *distract it with* divide it among. 323 *idleness* lack of cultiva-
tion. 324 *corrigible authority* corrective authority; ability to regulate the matter
[K]. 325-6 *If the balance . . . sensuality* Life is conceived of as a scale with
reason weighing down one side and sensuality the other. 326-7 *blood and base-*

seven years; and since I could distinguish betwixt a
benefit and an injury, I never found man that knew how
to love himself. Ere I would say I would drown myself
for the love of a guinea hen, I would change my human-
ity with a baboon.   315

ROD.   What should I do? I confess it is my shame to be so fond,
but it is not in my virtue to amend it.

IAGO.   Virtue? a fig! 'Tis in ourselves that we are thus or thus.
Our bodies are our gardens, to the which our wills are
gardeners; so that if we will plant nettles or sow lettuce, 320
set hyssop and weed up thyme, supply it with one gender
of herbs or distract it with many — either to have it
sterile with idleness or manured with industry — why,
the power and corrigible authority of this lies in our
wills. If the balance of our lives had not one scale of 325
reason to poise another of sensuality, the blood and
baseness of our natures would conduct us to most prepost'rous conclusions. But we have reason to cool our
raging motions, our carnal stings, our unbitted lusts;
whereof I take this that you call love to be a sect or 330
scion.

ROD.   It cannot be.

IAGO.   It is merely a lust of the blood and a permission of the
will. Come, be a man! Drown thyself? Drown cats and
blind puppies! I have profess'd me thy friend, and I 335
confess me knit to thy deserving with cables of perdurable toughness. I could never better stead thee than
now. Put money in thy purse. Follow these wars; defeat
thy favour with an usurp'd beard. I say, put money in

---

ness base passions.   328 *conclusions* results.   328–9 *we have reason . . . lusts*
Iago conceives of reason as the purely human ability to govern the passions by
control of will; its source is in the mind of man and not, as the more orthodox
believed, in a power above man.   *motions* impulses.   *unbitted* unbridled, uncon-
trolled.   330–1 *sect or scion* literally, a cutting or graft from a tree.   336 *knit to
thy deserving* bound to thee for favours received [K].   *perdurable* very durable
337 *stead* be of service to.   338–9 *defeat . . . usurp'd beard* spoil thy pretty face
by growing a beard to which it has no right [K].   *favour* face.

thy purse. It cannot be that Desdemona should long 340
continue her love to the Moor — put money in thy purse
— nor he his to her. It was a violent commencement, and
thou shalt see an answerable sequestration. Put but
money in thy purse. These Moors are changeable in
their wills. Fill thy purse with money. The food that to 345
him now is as luscious as locusts shall be to him shortly
as bitter as coloquintida. She must change for youth.
When she is sated with his body, she will find the error
of her choice. She must have change, she must. Therefore put money in thy purse. If thou wilt needs damn 350
thyself, do it a more delicate way than drowning. Make
all the money thou canst. If sanctimony and a frail vow
betwixt an erring barbarian and a supersubtle Venetian
be not too hard for my wits and all the tribe of hell,
thou shalt enjoy her. Therefore make money. A pox of 355
drowning thyself! It is clean out of the way. Seek thou
rather to be hang'd in compassing thy joy than to be
drown'd and go without her.

ROD.   Wilt thou be fast to my hopes, if I depend on the issue?

IAGO.   Thou art sure of me. Go, make money. I have told thee 360
often, and I retell thee again and again, I hate the Moor.
My cause is hearted; thine hath no less reason. Let us
be conjunctive in our revenge against him. If thou canst
cuckold him, thou dost thyself a pleasure, me a sport.
There are many events in the womb of time, which will 365
be delivered. Traverse! go! provide thy money! We will

---

343 *answerable sequestration* corresponding—and equally abrupt—estrangement
[K].   345 *wills* desires.   346 *locusts* probably St. John's bread, the fruit of the
locust tree; it is not likely that Iago is referring to the insect.   347 *coloquintida*
bitter apple or colocynth, a bitter fruit from which a medicinal purge was made.
349 *She must have change, she must* Q¹; not in F¹; omitted by some editors as a
probable memorial improvisation of "She must change for youth" (line 347) which
Q¹, in turn omits.   352 *sanctimony* the religious obligation of the marriage bond
[K].   353 *erring* wandering. *supersubtle* Iago does not mean that Desdemona is
more subtle than other Venetians, but that subtlety is a regular Venetian trait
[K].   356-7 *Seek thou . . . hang'd* if you wish to destroy yourself, take the risk of
being hanged for seducing the General's wife [K]. *compassing* achieving.   359
fast true.   362 *hearted* deeply fixed in my heart.   363 *conjunctive* united.
366 *Traverse* forward march.   370 *betimes* early.   371-4 *Go to . . . land* These

have more of this to-morrow. Adieu.

ROD.   Where shall we meet i' th' morning?

IAGO.   At my lodging.

ROD.   I'll be with thee betimes.   370

IAGO.   Go to, farewell. — Do you hear, Roderigo?

ROD.   What say you?

IAGO.   No more of drowning, do you hear?

ROD.   I am chang'd. I'll go sell all my land.   *Exit.*

IAGO.   Thus do I ever make my fool my purse;   375
For I mine own gain'd knowledge should profane
If I would time expend with such a snipe
But for my sport and profit. I hate the Moor;
And it is thought abroad that 'twixt my sheets
'Has done my office. I know not if't be true;   380
Yet I, for mere suspicion in that kind,
Will do as if for surety. He holds me well;
The better shall my purpose work on him.
Cassio's a proper man. Let me see now: *proper = handsome*
To get his place, and to plume up my will   385
In double knavery — How, how? Let's see.
After some time, to abuse Othello's ear
That he is too familiar with his wife.
He hath a person and a smooth dispose
To be suspected — fram'd to make women false.   390
The Moor is of a free and open nature
That thinks men honest that but seem to be so;

---

lines represent a conflation of the Q^1 and F^1 texts about which there has been
considerable disagreement among editors. Kittredge's arrangement is followed here.
377 *snipe* silly fellow (an extremely contemptuous term).   378–96 *I hate . . .
world's light* This is the soliloquy which Coleridge described as the "motive-hunting of motiveless malignity." Iago, however, lists several motives, including most
prominently his fears about Emilia.   379 *it is thought abroad* rumours are current.   381 *kind* regard.   382 *do as if for surety* act as though I were certain of it.
well in high regard.   384 *proper* handsome.   385 *plume up* gratify—literally,
deck with plumes (as a cap) [K].   387 *abuse* deceive.   389–90 *a smooth . . . be
suspected* a pleasant and affable disposition and manner, such as would make
one easily suspect him in such a case. This prepares us for the elegant and somewhat flourishing manners of Cassio [K].   391 *free* frank.

And will as tenderly be led by th' nose
As asses are.
I have't! It is engend'red! Hell and night   395
Must bring this monstrous birth to the world's light.

Exit.

---

393 *tenderly* easily, with little resistance.   395–6 *Hell and night . . . light* This is,
in effect, an invocation to the powers of evil to assist his plot [K].

Act Two

<><><><><><><><><><><><><><><><><><><><><><><><><><>

SCENE I. [*A seaport in Cyprus. An open place.*]

Enter Montano *and two* Gentlemen.

MON.   What from the cape can you discern at sea?

1. GENT.   Nothing at all. It is a high-wrought flood.
I cannot 'twixt the heaven and the main
Descry a sail.

MON.   Methinks the wind hath spoke aloud at land;   5
A fuller blast ne'er shook our battlements.
If it hath ruffian'd so upon the sea,
What ribs of oak, when mountains melt on them,
Can hold the mortise? What shall we hear of this?

2. GENT.   A segregation of the Turkish fleet.   10
For do but stand upon the foaming shore,
The chidden billow seems to pelt the clouds;
The wind-shak'd surge, with high and monstrous main,
Seems to cast water on the burning Bear
And quench the Guards of th' ever-fixed pole.   15

II.I. 1 *the cape* from which the Gentleman has just returned to bring his report to
Montano, who is in charge of affairs in Cyprus [K].   2 *high-wrought flood* high
and angry sea.   3 *main* sea.   7 *ruffian'd* raged.   9 *hold the mortise* hold together.   10 *segregation* dispersal.   12 *chidden* beaten (by the wind). Thus F¹; Q¹:
"chiding" is preferred by some editors.   13 *main* great body of waters (Q¹, F¹; KNIGHT,
K: "mane"). Knight's emendation, followed by Kittredge, would see in the line a
metaphoric allusion to the white horses of the sea. But the image of the horses
throwing water on the bear is somewhat ludicrous and un-Shakespearean. Since the
F¹, Q¹ reading makes perfect sense, there is no need to emend.   15 *the Guards*
two stars in the constellation of the Little Bear. The hyperbole in this description
of a storm follows an ancient literary convention [K].   *ever-fixed pole* North star.

31

I never did like molestation view
On the enchafed flood.

MON.   If that the Turkish fleet
Be not enshelter'd and embay'd, they are drown'd.
It is impossible they bear it out.

Enter a third Gentleman.

3. GENT. News, lads! Our wars are done.   20
The desperate tempest hath so bang'd the Turks
That their designment halts. A noble ship of Venice
Hath seen a grievous wrack and sufferance
On most part of their fleet.

MON. How? Is this true?

3. GENT.   The ship is here put in,   25
A Veronesa; Michael Cassio,
Lieutenant to the warlike Moor Othello,
Is come on shore; the Moor himself at sea,
And is in full commission here for Cyprus.

MON. I am glad on't. 'Tis a worthy governor.   30

3. GENT. But this same Cassio, though he speak of comfort
Touching the Turkish loss, yet he looks sadly
And prays the Moor be safe, for they were parted
With foul and violent tempest.

MON.   Pray heaven he be;
For I have serv'd him, and the man commands   35
Like a full soldier. Let's to the seaside, ho!
As well to see the vessel that's come in
As to throw out our eyes for brave Othello,
Even till we make the main and th' aerial blue

---

16 *like molestation* similar disturbance.   17 *enchafed flood* enraged ocean.   18 *embay'd* protected in a bay.   19 *bear it out* weather the storm.   22 *designment* plan, designs.   *halts* limps, is checked.   23 *wrack* wreck. *sufferance* disaster.   26 *Veronesa* Why Shakespeare should have Cassio, a Florentine from Venice, land in a ship of Verona, has puzzled editors. Perhaps it was a specific type of ship.   29 *in full . . . Cyprus* is on his way hither, to Cyprus, with a commission that gives him full power as Governor [K].   30 *worthy* honourable.   36 *full* perfect   39–40 *till we make . . . regard* so far out to sea that the blue water and the blue sky are no longer distinguishable from each other [K].   42 *arrivance* arrivals.   44 *approve*

An indistinct regard.

3. GENT.   Come, let's do so;   40
For every minute is expectancy
Of more arrivance.

       Enter Cassio.

CAS. Thanks you, the valiant of this warlike isle,
That so approve the Moor! O, let the heavens
Give him defence against the elements,   45
For I have lost him on a dangerous sea!

MON. Is he well shipp'd?

CAS. His bark is stoutly timber'd, and his pilot
Of very expert and approv'd allowance.
Therefore my hopes (not surfeited to death)   50
Stand in bold cure.
     (*Within*) "A sail, a sail, a sail!"

     Enter a Messenger.

CAS. What noise?

MESS. The town is empty; on the brow o' th' sea
Stand ranks of people, and they cry "A sail!"

CAS. My hopes do shape him for the Governor. *A shot.* 55

2. GENT. They do discharge their shot of courtesy.
Our friends at least.

CAS.   I pray you, sir, go forth
And give us truth who 'tis that is arriv'd.

2. GENT. I shall.   *Exit.*

MON. But, good Lieutenant, is your general wiv'd?   60

---

the Moor Cassio, as he advances from the rear of the stage, has heard Montano
praise Othello [K]. 49 *approv'd allowance* demonstrated ability. 50-1 *my hopes
. . . bold cure* Hope is surfeited to death when it has lasted so long that it changes
to despair. Cassio says that his hopes have not yet been indulged long enough to
reach this fatal stage; and that, though they are somewhat sick (mingled with
anxiety), they are in confident expectation of being cured (becoming a certainty,
being fulfilled). The figure is rather forced, but it accords with Cassio's elaborate
diction, which is that of an elegant Elizabethan gentleman [K]. 55 *shape . . .
Governor* wishfully imagine it to be the Governor's ship.

CAS.   Most fortunately. He hath achiev'd a maid
That paragons description and wild fame;
One that excels the quirks of blazoning pens,
And in th' essential vesture of creation
Does tire the ingener.

Enter Second Gentleman.

How now? Who has put in?   65

2. GENT.   'Tis one Iago, ancient to the General.

CAS.   Has had most favourable and happy speed.
Tempests themselves, high seas, and howling winds,
The gutter'd rocks and congregated sands,
Traitors ensteep'd to clog the guiltless keel,   70
As having sense of beauty, do omit
Their mortal natures, letting go safely by
The divine Desdemona.

MON.   What is she?

CAS.   She that I spake of, our great captain's captain,
Left in the conduct of the bold Iago,   75
Whose footing here anticipates our thoughts
A se'nnight's speed. Great Jove, Othello guard,
And swell his sail with thine own pow'rful breath,
That he may bless this bay with his tall ship,
Make love's quick pants in Desdemona's arms,   80
Give renew'd fire to our extincted spirits,
And bring all Cyprus comfort!

Enter Desdemona, Iago, Emilia, *and*
Roderigo, [*with* Attendants].

O, behold!

---

61 *achiev'd* won.   62 *paragons* surpasses.   *wild fame* rumour in her wildest mood,
when most given to exaggeration [K].   63 *excels . . . pens* is superior to any
flourishes that those who write in praise of her can make in their description [K].
64 *essential vesture of creation* real excellence with which God has created her.
65 *tire the ingener* wear out the most skilful contriver of compliments (K; F¹: "tyre
the Ingeniuer"; Q¹: "bear all excellency").   70 *ensteep'd* sunk in the sea.   71-2
omit . . . natures give up for the time being their deadly natures [K].   75 *conduct*
escort.   76-7 *Whose footing . . . speed* whose arrival is a week earlier than we
expected.   81 *extincted* despondent.   87 *enwheel* encircle.   93 *parted our fellow-*

The riches of the ship is come on shore!
Ye men of Cyprus, let her have your knees.
Hail to thee, lady! and the grace of heaven,   85
Before, behind thee, and on every hand,
Enwheel thee round!

DES.   I thank you, valiant Cassio.
What tidings can you tell me of my lord?

CAS.   He is not yet arriv'd; nor know I aught
But that he's well and will be shortly here.   90

DES.   O, but I fear! How lost you company?

CAS.   The great contention of the sea and skies
Parted our fellowship.

                (*Within*) "A sail, a sail!" [*A shot.*]

But hark. A sail!

2. GENT.   They give their greeting to the citadel.   95
This likewise is a friend.

CAS.   See for the news.

                [*Exit* Gentleman.]

Good ancient, you are welcome.
    Welcome, mistress. —   [*To* Emilia]
Let it not gall your patience, good Iago,
That I extend my manners. 'Tis my breeding
That gives me this bold show of courtesy.   [*Kisses her.*] 100

IAGO.   Sir, would she give you so much of her lips
As of her tongue she oft bestows on me,
You would have enough.

DES.   Alas, she has no speech!

---

ship separated our ships.   95 *give their greeting* by firing a shot.   98 *gall* irritate.
99 *extend my manners* give evidence of my courtesy.   100 *bold show of courtesy*
For Cassio to greet Emilia with a kiss was in accordance with Elizabethan custom.
Cassio speaks in a vein of persiflage. He has no fear that his action will gall Iago's
patience, nor is there anything "bold" about it [K].   103 *Alas, she has no speech*
Spoken in smiling protest. The whole of the dialogue that follows should be
spoken lightly. Iago's satire passes for mere badinage; though in fact, despite his
jesting air, it expresses, with a sincerity little suspected by his hearers, his real
opinion of human nature [K].

IAGO.	In faith, too much.
	I find it still when I have list to sleep. 105
	Marry, before your ladyship, I grant,
	She puts her tongue a little in her heart
	And chides with thinking.
EMIL.	You have little cause to say so.
IAGO.	Come on, come on! You are pictures out of doors, 110
	Bells in your parlours, wildcats in your kitchens,
	Saints in your injuries, devils being offended,
	Players in your housewifery, and housewives in your beds.
DES.	O, fie upon thee, slanderer!
IAGO.	Nay, it is true, or else I am a Turk. 115
	You rise to play, and go to bed to work.
EMIL.	You shall not write my praise.
IAGO.	No, let me not.
DES.	What wouldst thou write of me, if thou shouldst praise me?
IAGO.	O gentle lady, do not put me to't,
	For I am nothing if not critical. 120
DES.	Come on, assay. — There's one gone to the harbour?
IAGO.	Ay, madam.
DES.	I am not merry; but I do beguile
	The thing I am by seeming otherwise.
	Come, how wouldst thou praise me? 125

105 *still* always. *list* desire.   107–8 *puts her tongue . . . thinking* holds her tongue while she chides mentally.   110 *pictures* as pretty as pictures—with a suggestion that they owe their beauty to painting [K].   111 *Bells* with voices as sweet as bells.   112 *Saints in your injuries* when you injure anybody in speech or act, you do it with a saintly air [K].   113 *Players* triflers. *housewives* hussies.   114 *O, fie . . . slanderer* Iago's freedom of speech would not have offended the most fastidious lady of Shakespeare's time, if he spoke in jest. The way in which Desdemona smiles at his satire, and even encourages him to continue, proves that nobody takes his talk seriously [K].   117 *You shall . . . praise* when I want a complimentary copy of verses written I won't employ you [K].   120 *critical* censorious.   121 *assay* make the attempt. It was the fashion to compose verses extempore [K].   123–4 *beguile . . . otherwise* disguise my true feelings—perhaps out of anxiety for Othello—by seeming to be what I am not (merry).   127 *birdlime*

IAGO.   I am about it; but indeed my invention
        Comes from my pate as birdlime does from frieze —
        It plucks out brains and all. But my Muse labours,
        And thus she is deliver'd:

        If she be fair and wise, fairness and wit —   130
        The one's for use, the other useth it.

DES.   Well prais'd! How if she be black and witty?

IAGO.   If she be black, and thereto have a wit,
        She'll find a white that shall her blackness fit.

DES.   Worse and worse!   135

EMIL.   How if fair and foolish?

IAGO.   She never yet was foolish that was fair,
        For even her folly help'd her to an heir.

DES.   These are old fond paradoxes to make fools laugh i' th'
        alehouse. What miserable praise hast thou for her that's   140
        foul and foolish?

IAGO.   There's none so foul, and foolish thereunto,
        But does foul pranks which fair and wise ones do.

DES.   O heavy ignorance! Thou praisest the worst best. But
        what praise couldst thou bestow on a deserving woman   145
        indeed — one that, in the authority of her merit, did
        justly put on the vouch of very malice itself?

IAGO.   She that was ever fair, and never proud;
        Had tongue at will, and yet was never loud;

a sticky substance spread on bushes to catch small birds.   *frieze* coarse woolen
cloth.   129 *is deliver'd* gives birth.   132 *black* dark-haired or -complexioned.
134 *She'll find a white* even if she is not beautiful—for only blondes were admired
by the Elizabethans—yet she'll use her wits to find a fair lover. There may or may
not be a pun on "wight" [K].   138 *folly* (a) foolishness (b) unchastity.   139 *fond*
foolish.   141 *foul* ugly.   142 *thereunto* in addition.   144 *heavy* stupid.   145 *deserving woman* really praiseworthy woman. There is a wit combat between
Desdemona and Iago: his game is to describe all women in uncomplimentary
terms; hers is to propose as a subject for his verses a woman whom he cannot help
praising [K].   146–7 *in the authority . . . itself* by virtue of her admitted merit
did rightly prompt even the most malicious to testify in her favour [K].
149 *tongue at will* ability to express her feelings easily.

Never lack'd gold, and yet went never gay;   150
Fled from her wish, and yet said "Now I may";
She that, being ang'red, her revenge being nigh,
Bade her wrong stay, and her displeasure fly;
She that in wisdom never was so frail
To change the cod's head for the salmon's tail;   155
She that could think, and ne'er disclose her mind,
See suitors following, and not look behind:
She was a wight (if ever such wight were) —

DES.   To do what?

IAGO.   To suckle fools and chronicle small beer.   160

DES.   O most lame and impotent conclusion! Do not learn of
him, Emilia, though he be thy husband. How say you,
Cassio? Is he not a most profane and liberal counsellor?

CAS.   He speaks home, madam. You may relish him more in
the soldier than in the scholar.   165

IAGO.   [*aside*] He takes her by the palm. Ay, well said, whisper!
With as little a web as this will I ensnare as great a fly
as Cassio. Ay, smile upon her, do! I will gyve thee in
thine own courtship. You say true; 'tis so, indeed! If
such tricks as these strip you out of your lieutenantry,   170
it had been better you had not kiss'd your three fingers
so oft — which now again you are most apt to play the
sir in. Very good! well kiss'd! an excellent curtsy! 'Tis
so, indeed. Yet again your fingers to your lips? Would
they were clyster pipes for your sake! (*Trumpet within.*)   175
The Moor! I know his trumpet.

CAS.   'Tis truly so.

---

150 *gay* gorgeously dressed.   151 *Fled from . . . I may* refrained from doing something that she wished to do, though she knew that it was in her power to do it
[K].   152 *ang'red* offended.   *nigh* ready at hand.   153 *Bade . . . stay* chose to endure her injury.   155 *To change . . . tail* to exchange the best part of a cheap
fish for the worst part of an expensive one—to prefer ostentatious worthlessness to
homely excellence [K].   158 *wight* person.   160 *chronicle small beer* keep the
petty household accounts. Iago wins the game by saying that all this paragon is
good for is to act as nurse and housekeeper [K].   163 *liberal* licentious.   164
speaks home speaks directly and to the point.   164-5 *relish . . . scholar* prefer him

DES.   Let's meet him and receive him.

CAS.   Lo, where he comes!

Enter Othello *and* Attendants.

OTH.   O my fair warrior!

DES.   My dear Othello!   180

OTH.   It gives me wonder great as my content
       To see you here before me. O my soul's joy!
       If after every tempest come such calms,
       May the winds blow till they have waken'd death!
       And let the labouring bark climb hills of seas   185
       Olympus-high, and duck again as low
       As hell's from heaven! If it were now to die,
       'Twere now to be most happy; for I fear
       My soul hath her content so absolute
       That not another comfort like to this   190
       Succeeds in unknown fate.

DES.   The heavens forbid
       But that our loves and comforts should increase
       Even as our days do grow!

OTH.   Amen to that, sweet powers!
       I cannot speak enough of this content;
       It stops me here; it is too much of joy.   195
       And this, and this, the greatest discords be   *They kiss.*
       That e'er our hearts shall make!

IAGO.   [*aside*] O, you are well tun'd now!
       But I'll set down the pegs that make this music,
       As honest as I am.

OTH.   Come, let us to the castle.

---

more as a soldier than as a scholar (poet).   168 *gyve* ensnare (literally, with fetters).
169 *courtship* courtly manners.   172 *now* at this very moment.   172-3 *apt . . .
the sir* ready to act as a courtly gentleman.   175 *clyster pipes* medical syringes,
used primarily for enemas.   180 *O my fair warrior* This greeting recalls Desdemona's desire to share her husband's warlike life [K].   181 *content* happiness.
189 *absolute* perfect and complete.   195 *here* in his heart.   198 *set down the pegs*
The strings of some musical instruments were kept taut by means of pegs. To
loosen the pegs puts the instrument out of tune [K]. Iago will turn their harmony
into discord.

News, friends! Our wars are done; the Turks are
   drown'd.   200
How does my old acquaintance of this isle? —
Honey, you shall be well desir'd in Cyprus;
I have found great love amongst them. O my sweet,
I prattle out of fashion, and I dote
In mine own comforts. I prithee, good Iago,   205
Go to the bay and disembark my coffers.
Bring thou the master to the citadel.
He is a good one, and his worthiness
Does challenge much respect. — Come, Desdemona,
Once more well met at Cyprus.   210

                            Exeunt [all but Iago *and* Roderigo].

IAGO.   [*To an* Attendant, *who goes out*] Do thou meet me presently at the harbour. [*To* Roderigo] Come hither. If
thou be'st valiant (as they say base men being in love
have then a nobility in their natures more than is native
to them), list me. The Lieutenant to-night watches on   215
the court of guard. First, I must tell thee this: Desdemona is directly in love with him.

ROD.   With him? Why, 'tis not possible.

IAGO.   Lay thy finger thus, and let thy soul be instructed. Mark
me with what violence she first lov'd the Moor, but for   220
bragging and telling her fantastical lies; and will she
love him still for prating? Let not thy discreet heart
think it. Her eye must be fed; and what delight shall she
have to look on the devil? When the blood is made dull
with the act of sport, there should be, again to inflame   225

---

202 *well desir'd* warmly welcomed.   204 *out of fashion* unbecomingly.   205 *comforts* happiness.   206 *coffers* luggage.   207 *master* captain of the ship.   209 *challenge* claim, deserve.   211 *presently* at once.   215 *list* listen to.   216 *court of
guard* headquarters of the guard.   219 *thus* on the lips.   222 *still* forever.   *prating* speaking foolishly.   226 *favour* features.   227 *sympathy* agreement, correspond-
ence.   229 *requir'd conveniences* requisite points of fitness [K].   *tenderness* fastid-
iousness.   230 *abus'd* deceived.   *heave the gorge* suffer nausea.   233 *most pregnant . . . position* obvious and logical proposition.   234 *stands so eminent . . .
fortune* stands so high on the steps that lead to this good fortune [K].   235 *voluble*

it and to give satiety a fresh appetite, loveliness in favour, sympathy in years, manners, and beauties; all
which the Moor is defective in. Now for want of these
requir'd conveniences, her delicate tenderness will find
itself abus'd, begin to heave the gorge, disrelish and ab-   230
hor the Moor. Very nature will instruct her in it and
compel her to some second choice. Now, sir, this granted
(as it is a most pregnant and unforc'd position), who
stands so eminent in the degree of this fortune as
Cassio does? A knave very voluble; no further conscion-   235
able than in putting on the mere form of civil and humane seeming for the better compassing of his salt and
most hidden loose affection? Why, none! why, none! A
slipper and subtle knave; a finder-out of occasions; that
has an eye can stamp and counterfeit advantages, though   240
true advantage never present itself; a devilish knave!
Besides, the knave is handsome, young, and hath all
those requisites in him that folly and green minds look
after. A pestilent complete knave! and the woman hath
found him already.   245

ROD.   I cannot believe that in her. She's full of most blessed
condition.

IAGO.   Blessed fig's-end! The wine she drinks is made of grapes.
If she had been blessed, she would never have lov'd the
Moor. Blessed pudding! Didst thou not see her paddle   250
with the palm of his hand? Didst not mark that?

ROD.   Yes, that I did; but that was but courtesy.

IAGO.   Lechery, by this hand! an index and obscure prologue

---

fickle, easily changing. *conscionable* conscientious.   237 *compassing* attaining.
salt licentious.   238 *loose* lustful.   239 *slipper* slippery. *occasions* opportunities.
240 *stamp . . . advantages* craftily devise or contrive advantageous opportunities.
243 *green* inexperienced.   245 *found him* discovered what he is.   246–7 *blessed
condition* heavenly qualities.   248 *The wine . . . grapes* she is a human being,
not an angel, and so has the natural traits of mankind [K].   250 *pudding* sausage
(a contemptuous expression). *paddle* play suggestively.   253 *index* forerunner.
The index of a book was the "table of contents" which precedes the text of the
volume [K].

to the history of lust and foul thoughts. They met so
near with their lips that their breaths embrac'd together. 255
Villainous thoughts, Roderigo! When these mutualities
so marshal the way, hard at hand comes the master and
main exercise, th' incorporate conclusion. Pish! But, sir,
be you rul'd by me. I have brought you from Venice.
Watch you to-night; for the command, I'll lay't upon 260
you. Cassio knows you not. I'll not be far from you. Do
you find some occasion to anger Cassio, either by speaking too loud, or tainting his discipline, or from what
other course you please which the time shall more
favourably minister.   265

ROD.   Well.

IAGO.   Sir, he is rash and very sudden in choler, and haply
with his truncheon may strike at you. Provoke him that
he may; for even out of that will I cause these of Cyprus
to mutiny; whose qualification shall come into no true 270
taste again but by the displanting of Cassio. So shall you
have a shorter journey to your desires by the means I
shall then have to prefer them; and the impediment
most profitably removed without the which there were
no expectation of our prosperity.   275

ROD.   I will do this if you can bring it to any opportunity.

IAGO.   I warrant thee. Meet me by-and-by at the citadel. I must
fetch his necessaries ashore. Farewell.

ROD.   Adieu.   *Exit.*

---

256 *mutualities* reciprocal familiarities.   257 *marshal* lead. *hard at hand* soon
afterward.   258 *incorporate* united (by the joining of bodies).   263 *tainting* insulting.   265 *minister* provide.   267 *rash* hasty. *choler* anger. *haply* perhaps.
268 *truncheon* baton of office.   270–1 *whose qualification . . . Cassio* and they
will never be fully appeased unless Cassio is dismissed [K]. *qualification* appease-
ment, pacification   273 *prefer* forward.   276 *you* F¹; Q¹, K: "I." The tenour of
the passage indicates Roderigo's dependence upon Iago and thus supports the
F¹ reading.   277 *warrant thee* assure thee (that there will be an opportunity).
278 *his necessaries* Othello's luggage.   281 *apt* likely. *of great credit* very credible.
288 *led to diet* led on by the wish to feed—to glut or satisfy [K].   290 *leap'd into
my seat* The metaphor is from horsemanship.   294 *yet that* until.   297 *whom I
trash* whom I hold in check. To "trash" a hound in hunting is to hang clogs on his
collar to prevent him from outrunning the pack. (STEEVENS; F¹: "trace"; Q¹: "crush").

IAGO.   That Cassio loves her, I do well believe it;   280
That she loves him, 'tis apt and of great credit.
The Moor (howbeit that I endure him not)
Is of a constant, loving, noble nature,
And I dare think he'll prove to Desdemona
A most dear husband. Now I do love her too;   285
Not out of absolute lust (though peradventure
I stand accountant for as great a sin)
But partly led to diet my revenge,
For that I do suspect the lusty Moor
Hath leap'd into my seat; the thought whereof   290
Doth, like a poisonous mineral, gnaw my inwards;
And nothing can or shall content my soul
Till I am even'd with him, wife for wife;
Or failing so, yet that I put the Moor
At least into a jealousy so strong   295
That judgment cannot cure. Which thing to do,
If this poor trash of Venice, whom I trash
For his quick hunting, stand the putting on,
I'll have our Michael Cassio on the hip,
Abuse him to the Moor in the rank garb   300
(For I fear Cassio with my nightcap too),
Make the Moor thank me, love me, and reward me
For making him egregiously an ass
And practising upon his peace and quiet
Even to madness. 'Tis here, but yet confus'd.   305
Knavery's plain face is never seen till us'd.   *Exit.*

While Steevens' emendation has been generally accepted, some editors would read
"leash," which has essentially the same meaning.   298 *For his quick hunting* to
prevent him from running (hunting) too fast. *stand the putting on* be steadfast
(do not fail me) when I incite him to action (put him on).   299 *on the hip* in my
power. The term is from wrestling.   300 *Abuse* slander. *in the rank garb* in the
coarse fashion—by bringing the vilest kind of accusation against him [K].   304
practising upon plotting (successfully) against [K].   305 *yet confus'd* confused as
yet. Iago's plots develop as he takes advantage of one opportunity after another.
He adapts them to the moment. He sees the main points of what he wishes to
accomplish, but has not yet thought out the precise ways to fit them together [K].
306 *Knavery's . . . us'd* no knave sees his plan clearly in all its details until he
puts it into practice [K].

◆◇◆◇◆◇◆◇◆◇◆◇◆◇◆◇◆

SCENE II. [*Cyprus. A street.*]

Enter Othello's Herald, *reading a proclamation;* [*people following*].

HER. It is Othello's pleasure, our noble and valiant general,
that, upon certain tidings now arriv'd, importing the
mere perdition of the Turkish fleet, every man put himself into triumph; some to dance, some to make bonfires,
each man to what sport and revels his addiction leads   5
him. For, besides these beneficial news, it is the celebration of his nuptial. So much was his pleasure should be
proclaimed. All offices are open, and there is full liberty
of feasting from this present hour of five till the bell
have told eleven. Heaven bless the isle of Cyprus and   10
our noble general Othello!   *Exeunt.*

◆◇◆◇◆◇◆◇◆◇◆◇◆◇◆◇◆

[SCENE III. *Cyprus. A hall in the Castle.*]

Enter Othello, Desdemona, Cassio, *and* Attendants.

OTH. Good Michael, look you to the guard to-night.
Let's teach ourselves that honourable stop,
Not to outsport discretion.

CAS. Iago hath direction what to do;
But notwithstanding, with my personal eye   5
Will I look to't.

OTH.   Iago is most honest.
Michael, good night. To-morrow with your earliest
Let me have speech with you. — Come, my dear love.

II.II. 2 *upon* because of. 3 *mere perdition* utter destruction. 4 *triumph* joyous
celebration. 5 *addiction* inclination. 8 *offices* rooms where servants performed
their duties, served food and drink. *open* for food and drink. 10 *told* counted.
II.III. 3 *outsport discretion* celebrate to excess. 10 *profit's yet . . . and you*
The marriage has not yet been consummated. 14 *cast us* dismissed us. 19 *game*

The purchase made, the fruits are to ensue;
That profit's yet to come 'tween me and you. —   10
Good night.

         Exeunt Othello *and* Desdemona [*with*
         Attendants].
         Enter Iago.

CAS.   Welcome, Iago. We must to the watch.

IAGO.   Not this hour, Lieutenant; 'tis not yet ten o' th' clock.
Our general cast us thus early for the love of his Desdemona; who let us not therefore blame. He hath not   15
yet made wanton the night with her, and she is sport
for Jove.

CAS.   She's a most exquisite lady.

IAGO.   And I'll warrant her, full of game.

CAS.   Indeed, she's a most fresh and delicate creature.   20

IAGO.   What an eye she has! Methinks it sounds a parley to
provocation.

CAS.   An inviting eye; and yet methinks right modest.

IAGO.   And when she speaks, is it not an alarum to love?

CAS.   She is indeed perfection.   25

IAGO.   Well, happiness to their sheets! Come, Lieutenant, I
have a stoup of wine, and here without are a brace of
Cyprus gallants that would fain have a measure to the
health of black Othello.

CAS.   Not to-night, good Iago. I have very poor and unhappy   30
brains for drinking. I could well wish courtesy would
invent some other custom of entertainment.

IAGO.   O, they are our friends. But one cup! I'll drink for you.

---

love play.   21–2 *parley to provocation* literally, a call to battle, i.e. a summons to
the arms of love.   24 *alarum* summons. The military metaphor is continued.
27 *stoup* large cup, holding two quarts. *brace* pair.   28 *fain have a measure*
gladly drink a toast.   30 *unhappy* unfortunate.

CAS.   I have drunk but one cup to-night, and that was craftily
        qualified too; and behold what innovation it makes   35
        here. I am unfortunate in the infirmity and dare not
        task my weakness with any more.

IAGO.   What, man! 'Tis a night of revels. The gallants desire it.

CAS.   Where are they?

IAGO.   Here at the door. I pray you call them in.   40

CAS.   I'll do't, but it dislikes me.   *Exit.*

IAGO.   If I can fasten but one cup upon him
        With that which he hath drunk to-night already.
        He'll be as full of quarrel and offence
        As my young mistress' dog. Now my sick fool Roderigo,   45
        Whom love hath turn'd almost the wrong side out,
        To Desdemona hath to-night carous'd
        Potations pottle-deep; and he's to watch.
        Three lads of Cyprus — noble swelling spirits,
        That hold their honours in a wary distance,   50
        The very elements of this warlike isle —
        Have I to-night fluster'd with flowing cups,
        And they watch too. Now, 'mongst this flock of
            drunkards
        Am I to put our Cassio in some action
        That may offend the isle.

                    Enter Cassio, Montano, *and* Gentle-
                    men; [Servant *with wine*].

                            But here they come.   55
        If consequence do but approve my dream,
        My boat sails freely, both with wind and stream.

CAS.   Fore God, they have given me a rouse already.

34-5 *craftily qualified* diluted on the sly. *innovation* disturbance. 36 *here* with
a gesture indicating his head or face. 37 *task my weakness* burden (task) my poor
powers of resistance (with more than they can support). 41 *dislikes* displeases.
44 *offence* readiness to take offence. 48 *pottle-deep* as deep as the bottom of the
pottle. A "pottle" (literally, "little pot") was a big goblet. Every one of Roderigo's
healths has emptied his glass. This was a point of manners in old times [K].
49 *swelling* arrogant. 50 *That hold . . . wary distance* who are scrupulously
sensitive to even the remotest infringement on their personal honour [K]. 51 *very
elements* characteristic types—the individuals being warlike as the island itself is

MON.	Good faith, a little one; not past a pint, as I am a soldier.	60

IAGO. Some wine, ho!

[*Sings*]

> And let me the canakin clink, clink;
> And let me the canakin clink.
>   A soldier's a man;
>   O, man's life's but a span,   65
> Why then, let a soldier drink.

Some wine, boys!

CAS. Fore God, an excellent song!

IAGO. I learn'd it in England, where indeed they are most potent in potting. Your Dane, your German, and your   70 swag-bellied Hollander — Drink, ho! — are nothing to your English.

CAS. Is your Englishman so expert in his drinking?

IAGO. Why, he drinks you with facility your Dane dead drunk; he sweats not to overthrow your Almain; he gives your   75 Hollander a vomit ere the next pottle can be fill'd.

CAS. To the health of our General!

MON. I am for it, Lieutenant, and I'll do you justice.

IAGO. O sweet England!

[*Sings*]

> King Stephen was and a worthy peer;   80
>   His breeches cost him but a crown;
> He held 'em sixpence all too dear,
>   With that he call'd the tailor lown.

---

warlike.   53 *watch* are awake (when normally one should be in bed).   56 *If consequence . . . dream* if what follows only proves my expectation true [K]. 58 *rouse* bumper full of drink.   62 *canakin* small can.   70 *potent in potting* strong drinkers.   70-1 *Your Dane . . . Hollander* The Danes, the Germans, and the Dutch were proverbially hard drinkers [K].   75 *sweats not* need not exert himself. *Almain* German.   75-6 *gives . . . vomit* drinks enough to make a Dutchman throw up.   80-3 *King Stephen . . . lown* A stanza of an old song entitled "Bell my Wife," familiar to everybody in the audience [K].   *lown* rascal.

He was a wight of high renown,
    And thou art but of low degree.   85
'Tis pride that pulls the country down;
    Then take thine auld cloak about thee.

Some wine, ho!

CAS.   Fore God, this is a more exquisite song than the other.

IAGO.   Will you hear't again?   90

CAS.   No, for I hold him to be unworthy of his place that does
those things. Well, God's above all; and there be souls
must be saved, and there be souls must not be saved.

IAGO.   It's true, good Lieutenant.

CAS.   For mine own part — no offence to the General, nor any   95
man of quality — I hope to be saved.

IAGO.   And so do I too, Lieutenant.

CAS.   Ay, but, by your leave, not before me. The lieutenant is
to be saved before the ancient. Let's have no more of
this; let's to our affairs. God forgive us our sins! Gentle-   100
men, let's look to our business. Do not think, gentlemen,
I am drunk. This is my ancient. This is my right hand,
and this is my left. I am not drunk now. I can stand well
enough, and speak well enough.

ALL.   Excellent well!   105

CAS.   Why, very well then. You must not think then that I am
drunk.   *Exit.*

MON.   To th' platform, masters. Come, let's set the watch.

IAGO.   You see this fellow that is gone before.
He is a soldier fit to stand by Cæsar   110
And give direction; and do but see his vice.

---

86 *'Tis pride . . . down* it is extravagance in dress that causes hard times in our
country [K].   87 *Then take . . . thee* This is the substance of Bell's advice to
her husband in the interest of economy [K].   91 *place* position.   92–3 *there be
souls . . . not be saved* Cassio applies the doctrine of preordination to the question of propriety in the matter of drinking [K].   96 *quality* rank.   108 *platform*
the esplanade or paved court where the guard is mustered; the court of guard
[K].   *set the watch* mount the guard.   110 *stand by* act as right-hand man to.

'Tis to his virtue a just equinox,
The one as long as th' other. 'Tis pity of him.
I fear the trust Othello puts him in,
On some odd time of his infirmity,   115
Will shake this island.

MON.   But is he often thus?

IAGO.   'Tis evermore the prologue to his sleep.
He'll watch the horologe a double set
If drink rock not his cradle.

MON.   It were well
The General were put in mind of it.   120
Perhaps he sees it not, or his good nature
Prizes the virtue that appears in Cassio
And looks not on his evils. Is not this true?

Enter Roderigo.

IAGO.   [*aside to him*] How now, Roderigo?
I pray you after the Lieutenant, go!   *Exit* Roderigo. 125

MON.   And 'tis great pity that the noble Moor
Should hazard such a place as his own second
With one of an ingraft infirmity.
It were an honest action to say
So to the Moor.

IAGO.   Not I, for this fair island!   130
I do love Cassio well and would do much
To cure him of this evil.

                        (*Within*) "Help! help!"

                        But hark! What noise?

                Enter Cassio, *driving in* Roderigo.

CAS.   Zounds, you rogue! you rascal!

---

112 *just equinox* exact equivalent; it counterbalances his virtue just as night and
day are equal at the equinox.   115 *On some . . . infirmity* at some time or other
when this weakness of his has overcome him [κ].   118 *watch . . . double set* stay
awake for twenty-four hours.   119 *If drink . . . cradle* if drink has not put him
to sleep. The point is that Cassio cannot sleep without drinking first, according to
Iago.   122 *virtue* general excellence.   127 *second* second in command.   128 *ingraft* ingrafted, inveterate.

MON.   What's the matter, Lieutenant?

CAS.   A knave teach me my duty?
I'll beat the knave into a twiggen bottle.   135

ROD.   Beat me?

CAS.   Dost thou prate, rogue?   [*Strikes him.*]

MON.   Nay, good Lieutenant!   [*Stays him.*]
I pray you, sir, hold your hand.

CAS.   Let me go, sir,
Or I'll knock you o'er the mazzard.

MON.   Come, come, you're drunk!

CAS.   Drunk?

IAGO.   [*aside to* Roderigo] Away, I say! Go out and cry a
            mutiny!   *They fight.* 140

                        Exit Roderigo.

Nay, good Lieutenant. God's will, gentlemen!
Help, ho! — Lieutenant — sir — Montano — sir —
Help, masters! — Here's a goodly watch indeed!

                        A bell rung.

Who's that which rings the bell? Diablo, ho!
The town will rise. God's will, Lieutenant, hold!   145
You will be sham'd for ever.

                Enter Othello *and* Gentlemen *with
                weapons.*

OTH.   What is the matter here?

MON.   Zounds, I bleed still. I am hurt to the death. He dies!

                        [*Thrusts at* Cassio.]

---

135 *twiggen* covered with woven twigs of wicker work.   138 *mazzard* head.
140 *mutiny* riot.   144 *the bell* the alarum bell, which is rung because Roderigo
has cried "a mutiny" [K].   147 *He dies* F¹; not in Q¹, K.   *Thrusts at Cassio* The
stage direction is needed to indicate that Montano is speaking in anger. Kittredge
and some other editors, following Q², make a stage direction "He faints" of the
F¹ "He dies," but there is no reason to assume that this is not a part of Montano's
speech.   150 *place* position.   153 *do that* murder ourselves.   154 *forbid the
Ottomites* by wrecking the Turkish fleet.   156 *carve for his own rage* indulge his

OTH.	Hold for your lives!
IAGO.	Hold, hold! Lieutenant — sir — Montano — gentlemen!
	Have you forgot all sense of place and duty? 150
	Hold! The General speaks to you. Hold, hold, for shame!
OTH.	Why, how now, ho? From whence ariseth this?
	Are we turn'd Turks, and to ourselves do that
	Which heaven hath forbid the Ottomites?
	For Christian shame put by this barbarous brawl! 155
	He that stirs next to carve for his own rage
	Holds his soul light; he dies upon his motion.
	Silence that dreadful bell! It frights the isle
	From her propriety. What's the matter, masters?
	Honest Iago, that looks dead with grieving, 160
	Speak. Who began this? On thy love, I charge thee.
IAGO.	I do not know. Friends all but now, even now,
	In quarter, and in terms like bride and groom
	Devesting them for bed; and then, but now
	(As if some planet had unwitted men) 165
	Swords out, and tilting one at other's breast
	In opposition bloody. I cannot speak
	Any beginning to this peevish odds,
	And would in action glorious I had lost
	Those legs that brought me to a part of it! 170
OTH.	How comes it, Michael, you are thus forgot?
CAS.	I pray you pardon me. I cannot speak.
OTH.	Worthy Montano, you were wont be civil;
	The gravity and stillness of your youth
	The world hath noted, and your name is great 175
	In mouths of wisest censure. What's the matter

own rage in sword-play [ĸ].   157 *light* of slight value.   *motion* move.   159 *From her propriety* out of herself, out of her senses.   163 *In quarter* in friendship, observing each his proper station.   164 *Devesting* undressing.   165 *planet . . . men* It was commonly believed that the influence of certain planets, most notably the moon, could drive men to madness.   166 *tilting* thrusting.   168 *peevish odds* childish quarrel.   169 *in action glorious* on the battlefield.   171 *are thus forgot* have so forgotten yourself.   174 *stillness* sober behaviour.   175–6 *your name . . . censure* you have an excellent reputation among men of wise judgment.

That you unlace your reputation thus
And spend your rich opinion for the name
Of a night-brawler? Give me answer to't.

MON. Worthy Othello, I am hurt to danger. 180
Your officer, Iago, can inform you,
While I spare speech, which something now offends me,
Of all that I do know; nor know I aught
By me that's said or done amiss this night,
Unless self-charity be sometimes a vice, 185
And to defend ourselves it be a sin
When violence assails us.

OTH. Now, by heaven,
My blood begins my safer guides to rule,
And passion, having my best judgment collied,
Assays to lead the way. If I once stir 190
Or do but lift this arm, the best of you
Shall sink in my rebuke. Give me to know
How this foul rout began, who set it on;
And he that is approv'd in this offence,
Though he had twinn'd with me, both at a birth, 195
Shall lose me. What! in a town of war,
Yet wild, the people's hearts brimful of fear,
To manage private and domestic quarrel?
In night, and on the court and guard of safety?
'Tis monstrous. Iago, who began 't? 200

MON. If partially affin'd, or leagu'd in office,
Thou dost deliver more or less than truth,
Thou art no soldier.

IAGO. Touch me not so near.
I had rather have this tongue cut from my mouth
Than it should do offence to Michael Cassio. 205

---

177 *unlace* disorder, disgrace. 178 *spend* squander. *rich opinion* valuable reputation. *for* in exchange for. 182 *something* somewhat. *offends* hurts. Montano
means that he cannot speak without pain on account of his wound [K]. 185 *self-
charity* concern for one's self, self-defence. 188 *blood* anger. *safer guides* saner
judgment. 189 *collied* darkened (literally, blackened with coal). 190 *Assays* attempts. 193 *rout* brawl. 194 *approv'd in* found guilty of. 196 *town of war*
town under garrison. 198 *manage* carry on, engage in. *domestic* personal.

Yet I persuade myself, to speak the truth
Shall nothing wrong him. Thus it is, General.
Montano and myself being in speech,
There comes a fellow crying out for help,
And Cassio following him with determin'd sword   210
To execute upon him. Sir, this gentleman
Steps in to Cassio and entreats his pause.
Myself the crying fellow did pursue,
Lest by his clamour (as it so fell out)
The town might fall in fright. He, swift of foot,   215
Outran my purpose; and I return'd the rather
For that I heard the clink and fall of swords,
And Cassio high in oath; which till to-night
I ne'er might say before. When I came back
(For this was brief) I found them close together   220
At blow and thrust, even as again they were
When you yourself did part them.
More of this matter cannot I report;
But men are men; the best sometimes forget.
Though Cassio did some little wrong to him,   225
As men in rage strike those that wish them best,
Yet surely Cassio I believe receiv'd
From him that fled some strange indignity,
Which patience could not pass.

OTH.   I know, Iago,
Thy honesty and love doth mince this matter,   230
Making it light to Cassio. Cassio, I love thee;
But never more be officer of mine.

Enter Desdemona, *attended.*

Look if my gentle love be not rais'd up!
I'll make thee an example.

---

199 *on the court . . . safety* in the headquarters of the guard.   201 *affin'd* bound.
leagu'd in office prejudiced because he is your fellow officer.   211 *execute* carry
out his purpose.   212 *entreats his pause* pleads with him to stop.   214–15 *Lest
by his clamour . . . fright* This is Iago's only misrepresentation of any consequence
[K].   216 *the rather* all the sooner.   217 *For that* because.   218 *high in oath*
swearing loudly.   219 *might* could.   225 *him* Montano.   228 *indignity* insult.
229 *patience* self-control.   *pass* endure.   230 *mince* play down.

DES.   What's the matter?

OTH.   All's well now, sweeting; come away to bed.   235
        [*To* Montano] Sir, for your hurts, myself will be your
            surgeon.
        Lead him off.   [Montano *is led off.*]
        Iago, look with care about the town
        And silence those whom this vile brawl distracted.
        Come, Desdemona. 'Tis the soldiers' life   240
        To have their balmy slumbers wak'd with strife.

                    Exeunt [*all but* Iago *and* Cassio.]

IAGO.   What, are you hurt, Lieutenant?

CAS.   Ay, past all surgery.

IAGO.   Marry, God forbid!

CAS.   Reputation, reputation, reputation! O, I have lost my   245
        reputation! I have lost the immortal part of myself, and
        what remains is bestial. My reputation, Iago, my reputa-
        tion!

IAGO.   As I am an honest man, I thought you had receiv'd some
        bodily wound. There is more sense in that than in repu-   250
        tation. Reputation is an idle and most false imposition;
        oft got without merit and lost without deserving. You
        have lost no reputation at all unless you repute yourself
        such a loser. What, man! there are ways to recover the
        General again. You are but now cast in his mood — a   255
        punishment more in policy than in malice, even so as
        one would beat his offenceless dog to affright an imperi-
        ous lion. Sue to him again, and he's yours.

CAS.   I will rather sue to be despis'd than to deceive so good
        a commander with so slight, so drunken, and so indis-   260

---

235 *sweeting* sweetheart.   240 *'Tis the soldiers' life* this is the kind of life you
must expect if you wish to share my life as a soldier [K].   250 *sense* feeling.
251 *imposition* that which is placed upon a man by others.   254 *recover* win back.
255 *cast* dismissed. *in his mood* as a result of his anger.   256 *more in policy than
in malice* inflicted rather because he thinks it good policy to punish you (for the
maintenance of discipline) than because he feels any ill will toward you [K].
257–8 *beat his . . . imperious lion* punish an insignificant person to warn an important one against doing wrong (an old proverb).   258 *Sue* appeal.   260 *slight*

creet an officer. Drunk? and speak parrot? and squabble?
swagger? swear? and discourse fustian with one's own
shadow? O thou invisible spirit of wine, if thou hast no
name to be known by, let us call thee devil!

IAGO.   What was he that you follow'd with your sword? What 265
had he done to you?

CAS.   I know not.

IAGO.   Is't possible?

CAS.   I remember a mass of things, but nothing distinctly; a
quarrel, but nothing wherefore. O God, that men should 270
put an enemy in their mouths to steal away their brains!
that we should with joy, pleasance, revel, and applause
transform ourselves into beasts!

IAGO.   Why, but you are now well enough. How came you thus
recovered?
275

CAS.   It hath pleas'd the devil drunkenness to give place to the
devil wrath. One unperfectness shows me another, to
make me frankly despise myself.

IAGO.   Come, you are too severe a moraler. As the time, the
place, and the condition of this country stands, I could 280
heartily wish this had not so befall'n; but since it is as
it is, mend it for your own good.

CAS.   I will ask him for my place again: he shall tell me I am
a drunkard! Had I as many mouths as Hydra, such an
answer would stop them all. To be now a sensible man, 285
by-and-by a fool, and presently a beast! O strange! Every
inordinate cup is unblest, and the ingredience is a devil.

IAGO.   Come, come, good wine is a good familiar creature if it

---

worthless (F¹; Q¹: "light"). Some editors prefer the Q¹ reading as meaning "irrespon-
sible."   261 *speak parrot* talk nonsense, without knowing what one is saying.
262 *fustian* nonsense. The word originally was the name of a coarse kind of cloth,
like corduroy.   277 *unperfectness* imperfection, weakness.   278 *frankly* without
reserve.   284 *Hydra* the many-headed serpent of Greek mythology, destroyed by
Hercules; when one head was cut off, two new ones sprang out to replace it.
287 *inordinate* beyond moderation.   *ingredience* contents.   288 *familiar* useful.

be well us'd. Exclaim no more against it. And, good
Lieutenant, I think you think I love you.   290

CAS.   I have well approv'd it, sir. I drunk?

IAGO.   You or any man living may be drunk at a time, man.
I'll tell you what you shall do. Our General's wife is now
the General. I may say so in this respect, for that he hath
devoted and given up himself to the contemplation, 295
mark, and denotement of her parts and graces. Confess
yourself freely to her. Importune her help to put you in
your place again. She is of so free, so kind, so apt, so
blessed a disposition she holds it a vice in her goodness
not to do more than she is requested. This broken joint 300
between you and her husband entreat her to splinter;
and my fortunes against any lay worth naming, this
crack of your love shall grow stronger than 'twas before.

CAS.   You advise me well.

IAGO.   I protest, in the sincerity of love and honest kindness.   305

CAS.   I think it freely; and betimes in the morning will I beseech the virtuous Desdemona to undertake for me. I
am desperate of my fortunes if they check me here.

IAGO.   You are in the right. Good night, Lieutenant. I must to
the watch.   310

CAS.   Good night, honest Iago.   *Exit.*

IAGO.   And what's he then that says I play the villain,
When this advice is free I give and honest,
Probal to thinking, and indeed the course

---

291 *approv'd it* found it true by experience.   294 *for that* because.   296 *parts*
accomplishment.   *graces* charms.   298 *free* bounteous.   *apt* ready (to do kindness).
300 *joint* relationship.   301 *splinter* bind with splints. The metaphor is from the
practice of surgery.   302 *lay* wager, stake.   303 *crack . . . before* It was an old
notion that a broken bone mended would be stronger than it was before the break.
Thus the surgical metaphor is carried on.   306 *betimes* early.   308 *desperate*
hopeless.   *check me* fail me.   314 *Probal to thinking* such as would be approved
by good judgment [K].   316 *inclining* inclining by nature to do what is asked
of her [K].   *subdue* persuade.   317 *fruitful* generous.   320 *All seals . . . redeemed*
sin Baptism is the seal (or confirmation) of a man's redemption from sin; and,
being a rite of purification, is also a symbol of restoration to innocence. "Seals
and symbols" is in a kind of apposition with "baptism":—"to renounce his bap-

To win the Moor again? For 'tis most easy   315
Th' inclining Desdemona to subdue
In any honest suit. She's fram'd as fruitful
As the free elements. And then for her
To·win the Moor — were't to renounce his baptism —
All seals and symbols of redeemed sin —   320
His soul is so enfetter'd to her love
That she may make, unmake, do what she list,
Even as her appetite shall play the god
With his weak function. How am I then a villain
To counsel Cassio to this parallel course,   325
Directly to his good? Divinity of hell!
When devils will the blackest sins put on,
They do suggest at first with heavenly shows,
As I do now. For whiles this honest fool
Plies Desdemona to repair his fortunes,   330
And she for him pleads strongly to the Moor,
I'll pour this pestilence into his ear —
That she repeals him for her body's lust;
And by how much she strives to do him good,
She shall undo her credit with the Moor.   335
So will I turn her virtue into pitch,
And out of her own goodness make the net
That shall enmesh them all.

Enter Roderigo.

How now, Roderigo?

ROD.   I do follow here in the chase, not like a hound that

---

tism—yes, and whatever other seals and symbols of redemption there are in Chris-
tianity" [K].   323 *her appetite* his sexual desire for her.   *play the god* rule abso-
lutely.   324 *weak function* human powers of mind and body, specifically his sexual
power which, since Othello is old, Iago regards as inadequate to satisfy Desdemona.   325 *parallel* leading to the same end, Othello's destruction.   326 *Directly
to* in complete accord with.   *Divinity of hell* the kind of theological reasoning
(divinity) which a devil might use.   327 *put on* instigate.   328 *suggest* tempt.
heavenly shows mere appearances of holiness.   330 *Plies* urges.   333 *repeals* is
trying to procure his recall.   335 *undo her credit* destroy her reputation.   336
pitch (a) blackness (b) that which has the power to ensnare, as pitch was sometimes used because of its viscous quality.

hunts, but one that fills up the cry. My money is almost 340
spent; I have been tonight exceedingly well cudgell'd;
and I think the issue will be — I shall have so much experience for my pains; and so, with no money at all, and
a little more wit, return again to Venice.

IAGO.   How poor are they that have not patience!   345
What wound did ever heal but by degrees?
Thou know'st we work by wit, and not by witchcraft;
And wit depends on dilatory time.
Does't not go well? Cassio hath beaten thee,
And thou by that small hurt hast cashier'd Cassio.   350
Though other things grow fair against the sun,
Yet fruits that blossom first will first be ripe.
Content thyself awhile. By th' mass, 'tis morning!
Pleasure and action make the hours seem short.
Retire thee; go where thou art billeted.   355
Away, I say! Thou shalt know more hereafter.
Nay, get thee gone!   *Exit* Roderigo.
                    Two things are to be done:
My wife must move for Cassio to her mistress;
I'll set her on;
Myself the while to draw the Moor apart   360
And bring him jump when he may Cassio find
Soliciting his wife. Ay, that's the way!
Dull not device by coldness and delay.   *Exit.*

---

340 *fills up the cry* merely makes up one of the pack.   344 *wit* intelligence.
347 *wit* clever planning.   350 *cashier'd Cassio* procured Cassio's dismissal. Iago
plays on words contemptuously [K].   351-2 *Though other things . . . be ripe* even
though our other plans (your attaining of Desdemona) are developing favourably,
the more immediate steps (the dismissal of Cassio) must be accomplished before
we can attain the ultimate goal; first things must come first.   355 *billeted* quar-
tered. The "billet" is the "little bill" or document designating the person at whose
house a soldier is to lodge [K].   358 *move* plead.   361 *jump* exactly at the right
time.   363 *device* strategy. *coldness* lack of energy, sluggishness.

Act Three

◇◇

SCENE I. [*Cyprus. Before the Castle.*]

Enter Cassio, *with* Musicians.

CAS. Masters, play here, I will content your pains:
Something that's brief; and bid "Good morrow,
General."   *They play.*

Enter the Clown.

CLOWN. Why, masters, have your instruments been at Naples,
that they speak i' th' nose thus?

MUS. How, sir, how?   5

CLOWN. Are these, I pray, call'd wind instruments?

MUS. Ay, marry, are they, sir.

CLOWN. O, thereby hangs a tail.

MUS. Whereby hangs a tale, sir?

CLOWN. Marry, sir, by many a wind instrument that I know.   10
But, masters, here's money for you; and the General so
likes your music that he desires you, of all loves, to
make no more noise with it.

III.I. 1 *play here* Such a greeeting of music to the newly married was a courteous custom. The dramatic purpose of the episode is to make an interval in the main action before the reappearance of Iago [K]. *content your pains* reward you for your trouble.   3-4 *Naples . . . nose thus* This obviously bawdy reference has never been satisfactorily explained. Naples was known as the center of venereal disease. The clown seems to be criticizing the music as sounding like the speech of sufferers from this malady.   8 *tail* slang for penis.   10 *wind instrument* buttocks, capable of producing wind.   12 *of all loves* for the sake of any affection you may feel for him [K].   15 *to't* go to it.

MUS.	Well, sir, we will not.
CLOWN.	If you have any music that may not be heard, to't again. 15
	But, as they say, to hear music the General does not greatly care.
MUS.	We have none such, sir.
CLOWN.	Then put up your pipes in your bag, for I'll away.
	Go, vanish into air, away! *Exeunt* Musicians. 20
CAS.	Dost thou hear, my honest friend?
CLOWN.	No, I hear not your honest friend. I hear you.
CAS.	Prithee keep up thy quillets. There's a poor piece of gold for thee. If the gentlewoman that attends the General's wife be stirring, tell her there's one Cassio entreats 25 her a little favour of speech. Wilt thou do this?
CLOWN.	She is stirring, sir. If she will stir hither, I shall seem to notify unto her.
CAS.	Do, good my friend. *Exit* Clown.

Enter Iago.

In happy time, Iago.

IAGO.	You have not been abed then? 30
CAS.	Why, no. The day had broke
	Before we parted. I have made bold, Iago,
	To send in to your wife. My suit to her
	Is that she will to virtuous Desdemona
	Procure me some access.
IAGO.	I'll send her to you presently; 35
	And I'll devise a mean to draw the Moor
	Out of the way, that your converse and business
	May be more free.
CAS.	I humbly thank you for't. *Exit* [Iago].

22 *No, I hear . . . you* A common form of Elizabethan humour known as equivocation.   23 *keep up* keep to yourself. *quillets* quips, puns.   27 *seem to* arrange to.   29 *In happy time* well met.   36 *mean* means.   37 *converse* conversation. 40 *A Florentine* even a Florentine, as Cassio himself is; Iago, of course, is a Venetian.   42 *displeasure* being out of favour.   46 *affinity* family connections. *in wholesome wisdom* out of a prudent regard for good policy [K].   48 *likings*

                                    I never knew
         A Florentine more kind and honest.   40

                        Enter Emilia.

EMIL.   Good morrow, good Lieutenant. I am sorry
         For your displeasure; but all will sure be well.
         The General and his wife are talking of it,
         And she speaks for you stoutly. The Moor replies
         That he you hurt is of great fame in Cyprus   45
         And great affinity, and that in wholesome wisdom
         He might not but refuse you. But he protests he loves
              you,
         And needs no other suitor but his likings
         To take the safest occasion by the front
         To bring you in again.

CAS.   Yet I beseech you,   50
         If you think fit, or that it may be done,
         Give me advantage of some brief discourse
         With Desdemona alone.

EMIL.   Pray you come in.
         I will bestow you where you shall have time
         To speak your bosom freely.

CAS.   I am much bound to you.   *Exeunt.* 55

◇◇◇◇◇◇◇◇◇◇◇◇◇◇◇

SCENE II. [*Cyprus. A room in the Castle.*]

Enter Othello, Iago, *and* Gentlemen.

OTH.   These letters give, Iago, to the pilot
         And by him do my duties to the state.
         That done, I will be walking on the works.

affections.   49 *occasion* opportunity. *front* forehead; forelock. Occasion (like
Time and Fortune) was described and figured as bald except for one long lock on
the forehead. Shakespeare remembered the proverb as he had read it in the so-
called DISTICHA CATONIS, ii, 26—a primary schoolbook in his time [K]. The proverb
occurs very often in Elizabethan literature.   54 *bestow* place.

Repair there to me.

IAGO.   Well, my good lord, I'll do't.

OTH.   This fortification, gentlemen, shall we see't?   5

GENT.   We'll wait upon your lordship.   *Exeunt.*

◇◇◇◇◇◇◇◇◇◇◇◇◇◇◇◇◇   *Attention to relationship*
The Temptation Scene

SCENE III. [*Cyprus. The garden of the Castle.*]

Enter Desdemona, Cassio, *and* Emilia.

DES.   Be thou assur'd, good Cassio, I will do
All my abilities in thy behalf.

EMIL.   Good madam, do. I warrant it grieves my husband
As if the cause were his.

DES.   O, that's an honest fellow. Do not doubt, Cassio,   5
But I will have my lord and you again
As friendly as you were.

CAS.   Bounteous madam,
Whatever shall become of Michael Cassio,
He's never anything but your true servant.

DES.   I know't; I thank you. You do love my lord;   10
You have known him long; and be you well assur'd
He shall in strangeness stand no farther off
Than in a politic distance.

CAS.   Ay, but, lady,

III.II. The purpose of this scene is to explain the absence of Othello during Cassio's interview with Desdemona. Iago meant "to draw the Moor out of the way" (III.1.36–7) ; but apparently luck had played into his hand and no "device" was necessary. Certain gentlemen of Cyprus had called upon Othello, with whom he thought it necessary to inspect some part of the fortifications ("the works") [K]. 2 *do my duties* pay my respects.   4 *Repair* come.

III.III. The short scene that precedes has given Emilia time to conduct Cassio to her mistress. Scene III opens in the midst of the conversation. Cassio has already made his petition to Desdemona [K]. This "temptation" scene is the pivotal scene of the play, in which Othello is forced to choose between Iago and Desdemona. At the beginning he is the self-sufficient master of his passions; at the

That policy may either last so long,
Or feed upon such nice and waterish diet,   15
Or breed itself so out of circumstance,
That, I being absent, and my place supplied,
My general will forget my love and service.

DES.   Do not doubt that. Before Emilia here
I give thee warrant of thy place. Assure thee,   20
If I do vow a friendship, I'll perform it
To the last article. My lord shall never rest;
I'll watch him tame and talk him out of patience;
His bed shall seem a school, his board a shrift;
I'll intermingle everything he does   25
With Cassio's suit. Therefore be merry, Cassio,
For thy solicitor shall rather die
Than give thy cause away.

Enter Othello *and* Iago.

EMIL.   Madam, here comes my lord.

CAS.   Madam, I'll take my leave.   30

DES.   Why, stay, and hear me speak.

CAS.   Madam, not now. I am very ill at ease.
Unfit for mine own purposes.

DES.   Well, do your discretion.   *Exit* Cassio.

IAGO.   Ha! I like not that.

OTH.   What dost thou say?   35

IAGO.   Nothing, my lord; or if — I know not what.

OTH.   Was not that Cassio parted from my wife?

---

end he is an inhuman monster, ravaged by jealousy, completely in the power of
Iago.   12–13 *He shall . . . politic distance* his estrangement will assuredly last no
longer than policy requires [K].   15 *feed upon . . . diet* be kept alive by such
trivial and insignificant considerations [K].   16 *breed . . . circumstance* perpetu-
ate itself by new circumstances which may occur.   17 *place supplied* position oc-
cupied (by another).   19 *doubt* fear.   20 *warrant* promise.   23 *watch him tame*
tame him by keeping him awake. An allusion to the method of taming falcons [K].
24 *shrift* confessional, where one has to listen to the admonitions of the priest
[K].   26 *merry* cheerful.   28 *give thy cause away* abandon it.   35 *I like not that*
Iago takes instant advantage of Cassio's hurried departure. He utilizes every
chance occurrence [K]. With this line the temptation of Othello begins.

IAGO.   Cassio, my lord? No, sure, I cannot think it,
That he would steal away so guilty-like,
Seeing you coming.

OTH.   I do believe 'twas he.   40

DES.   How now, my lord?
I have been talking with a suitor here,
A man that languishes in your displeasure.

OTH.   Who is't you mean?

DES.   Why, your lieutenant, Cassio. Good my lord,   45
If I have any grace or power to move you,
His present reconciliation take;
For if he be not one that truly loves you,
That errs in ignorance, and not in cunning,
I have no judgment in an honest face.   50
I prithee call him back.

OTH.   Went he hence now?

DES.   Yes, faith; so humbled
That he hath left part of his grief with me
To suffer with him. Good love, call him back.

OTH.   Not now, sweet Desdemona; some other time.   55

DES.   But shall't be shortly?

OTH.   The sooner, sweet, for you.

DES.   Shall't be to-night at supper?

OTH.   No, not to-night.

DES.   To-morrow dinner then?

OTH.   I shall not dine at home.
I meet the captains at the citadel.

---

46 *grace* favour in your eyes.   47 *reconciliation* repentance with the hope of
reconciliation.   *take* accept.   49 *in cunning* knowingly, on purpose.   55 *some
other time* Othello has no suspicions as yet; nor is he either displeased or impatient. He is simply very busy, and not quite ready to receive Cassio [K]. Although
Iago's subtle insinuations had begun at line 34, Othello is not abnormally jealous,
and it will take much more provocation before he begins to fall.   58 *dinner* the

DES.   Why then, to-morrow night, or Tuesday morn,   60
Or Tuesday noon or night, or Wednesday morn.
I prithee name the time, but let it not
Exceed three days. I' faith, he's penitent;
And yet his trespass, in our common reason
(Save that, they say, the wars must make examples   65
Out of their best) is not almost a fault
T' incur a private check. When shall he come?
Tell me, Othello. I wonder in my soul
What you could ask me that I should deny
Or stand so mamm'ring on. What? Michael Cassio   70
That came a-wooing with you, and so many a time,
When I have spoke of you dispraisingly,
Hath ta'en your part — to have so much to do
To bring him in? Trust me, I could do much —

[margin handwritten note: othello laughing at various times]

OTH.   Prithee no more. Let him come when he will!   75
I will deny thee nothing.

DES.   Why, this is not a boon.
'Tis as I should entreat you wear your gloves,
Or feed on nourishing dishes, or keep you warm,
Or sue to you to do a peculiar profit
To your own person. Nay, when I have a suit   80
Wherein I mean to touch your love indeed,
It shall be full of poise and difficult weight,
And fearful to be granted.

OTH.   I will deny thee nothing!
Whereon I do beseech thee grant me this,
To leave me but a little to myself.   85

DES.   Shall I deny you? No. Farewell, my lord.

OTH.   Farewell, my Desdemona. I'll come to thee straight.

DES.   Emilia, come. — Be as your fancies teach you.

---

noonday meal.   64 *in our common reason* if judged as we ordinarily regard such things [K].   65–6 *the wars . . . their best* military discipline demands that the best man be sometimes punished as examples to the others.   66 *their* ROWE; F[1], Q[1]: "her." *not almost* hardly.   67 *private check* personal rebuke.   70 *mamm'ring* hesitating.   79 *peculiar* personal.   81 *touch* test.   82 *poise* weight.   87 *straight* soon.   88 *fancies* inclinations. *teach* guide.

Whate'er you be, I am obedient.

Exeunt Desdemona *and* Emilia.

OTH.   Excellent wretch! Perdition catch my soul   90
But I do love thee! and when I love thee not,
Chaos is come again.

IAGO.   My noble lord —

OTH.   What dost thou say, Iago?

IAGO.   Did Michael Cassio, when you woo'd my lady,
Know of your love?   95

OTH.   He did, from first to last. Why dost thou ask?

IAGO.   But for a satisfaction of my thought;
No further harm.

OTH.   Why of thy thought, Iago?

IAGO.   I did not think he had been acquainted with her.

OTH.   O, yes, and went between us very oft.   100

IAGO.   Indeed?

OTH.   Indeed? Ay, indeed! Discern'st thou aught in that?
Is he not honest?

IAGO.   Honest, my lord?

OTH.   Honest? Ay, honest.

IAGO.   My lord, for aught I know.

OTH.   What dost thou think?

91–2 *and when I love . . . come again* I shall love thee as long as the universe
lasts. Nothing shall put an end to my love but the universal return to chaos which
is to mark the end of time. This speech is sometimes strangely misunderstood, as
if Othello meant that, if anything should cause him to cease to love her, the result would be chaos. But Othello is in no questioning mood; he is not contem-
plating the possibility of ceasing to love Desdemona, but emphasizing its impossi-
bility. By-and-by, when the catastrophe comes, we are at liberty to remember his
words and, if we like, to perceive that they were, if taken in a sense not meant by
him, a prophecy of coming ruin. This tragic irony was doubtless intentional on
Shakespeare's part [K].   94–5 *Did Michael . . . of your love* Iago now resumes
the assault, recalling the remark which Othello seems to have forgotten.   96 *Why
dost thou ask* Iago has succeeded in arousing Othello's curiosity and thus to lead
him into discussion.   103 *honest* honourable.   107–8 *As if . . . to be shown* Iago

IAGO.   Think, my lord?

OTH.   Think, my lord? 105
By heaven, he echoes me,
As if there were some monster in his thought
Too hideous to be shown. Thou dost mean something.
I heard thee say even now, thou lik'st not that,
When Cassio left my wife. What didst not like?   110
And when I told thee he was of my counsel
In my whole course of wooing, thou cried'st "Indeed?"
And didst contract and purse thy brow together,
As if thou then hadst shut up in thy brain
Some horrible conceit. If thou dost love me,   115
Show me thy thought.

IAGO.   My lord, you know I love you.

OTH.   I think thou dost;
And, for I know thou'rt full of love and honesty
And weigh'st thy words before thou giv'st them breath,
Therefore these stops of thine fright me the more;   120
For such things in a false disloyal knave
Are tricks of custom; but in a man that's just
They are close dilations, working from the heart
That passion cannot rule.

IAGO.   For Michael Cassio,
I dare be sworn I think that he is honest.   125

OTH.   I think so too.

IAGO.   Men should be what they seem;

---

has now fully aroused Othello into active consideration of the possibility of some
evil unknown to him. He now reviews all of the stages of Iago's assault and demands further elucidation.   111 *of my counsel* in my confidence.   115 *conceit*
conception, idea.   120 *stops* pauses, hesitations.   122 *tricks of custom* usual char-
acteristics.   123–4 *They are close dilations . . . cannot rule* they are secret
emotions, forcing their way from the speaker's very heart, which cannot control
its agitation. The man's heart is stirred by some horrible thought which he wishes
to conceal, but, though he controls his tongue, he cannot prevent the emotions of
his heart from interrupting speech [K]. *dilations* swellings (F¹; Q¹: "denotements").
The meaning has been much disputed; some editors prefer the Q¹ reading and
some Steevens' emendation, "delations," meaning "spyings." Kittredge is probably
correct.

	Or those that be not, would they might seem none!	
OTH.	Certain, men should be what they seem.	
IAGO.	Why then, I think Cassio's an honest man.	
OTH.	Nay, yet there's more in this.	130
	I prithee speak to me, as to thy thinkings,	
	As thou dost ruminate, and give thy worst of thoughts	
	The worst of words.	
IAGO.	Good my lord, pardon me.	
	Though I am bound to every act of duty,	
	I am not bound to that all slaves are free to.	135
	Utter my thoughts? Why, say they are vile and false,	
	As where's that palace whereinto foul things	
	Sometimes intrude not? Who has a breast so pure	
	But some uncleanly apprehensions	
	Keep leets and law days, and in session sit	140
	With meditations lawful?	
OTH.	Thou dost conspire against thy friend, Iago,	
	If thou but think'st him wrong'd, and mak'st his ear	
	A stranger to thy thoughts.	
IAGO.	I do beseech you —	
	Though I perchance am vicious in my guess	145
	(As I confess it is my nature's plague	
	To spy into abuses, and oft my jealousy	
	Shapes faults that are not), that your wisdom yet	
	From one that so imperfectly conceits	
	Would take no notice, nor build yourself a trouble	150
	Out of his scattering and unsure observance.	

---

127 *would they might seem none* would they might not seem to be men at all (but monsters, as they really are) [K]. Iago is suggesting that Cassio's is only a seeming virtue and vehemently lamenting that this should be so.   131-2 *speak to me . . . dost ruminate* tell me thy thoughts exactly as thou dost think them [K]. 135 *bound to . . . free to* obliged to do even what slaves are not obliged to do, utter my thoughts.   137-8 *As where's . . . intrude not* just as foul things sometimes intrude into the most splendid palace, so vile and false thoughts come now and then, unbidden, into the purest breast. Iago contrives to assert his well-known "honesty" even in the act of admitting that he entertains suspicions which may be "vile and false" [K].   139 *apprehensions* thoughts.   140 *leets* court sessions.   145 *vicious in my guess* mistaken (literally, faulty) in what I suspect [K]. 147 *jealousy* tendency to scrutinize closely and carefully.   149 *so imperfectly con-*

	It were not for your quiet nor your good,	
	Nor for my manhood, honesty, or wisdom,	
	To let you know my thoughts.	
OTH.	What dost thou mean?	
IAGO.	Good name in man and woman, dear my lord,	155
	Is the immediate jewel of their souls.	
	Who steals my purse steals trash; 'tis something, nothing;	
	'Twas mine, 'tis his, and has been slave to thousands;	
	But he that filches from me my good name	
	Robs me of that which not enriches him	160
	And makes me poor indeed.	
OTH.	By heaven, I'll know thy thoughts!	
IAGO.	You cannot, if my heart were in your hand;	
	Nor shall not whilst 'tis in my custody.	
OTH.	Ha!	
IAGO.	O, beware, my lord, of jealousy!	165
	It is the green-ey'd monster, which doth mock	
	The meat it feeds on. That cuckold lives in bliss	
	Who, certain of his fate, loves not his wronger;	
	But O, what damned minutes tells he o'er	
	Who dotes, yet doubts — suspects, yet strongly loves!	170
OTH.	O misery!	
IAGO.	Poor and content is rich, and rich enough;	
	But riches fineless is as poor as winter	
	To him that ever fears he shall be poor.	
	Good heaven, the souls of all my tribe defend	175

ceits has such vague, unformed ideas on the subject [K].   151 *scattering* random. *observance* observation.   156 *immediate jewel of* treasure closest to.   162 *By heaven . . . thoughts* Iago's little homily on reputation has served to raise Othello's curiosity and fear to a fever pitch.   165 *O, beware . . . of jealousy* Here, for the first time, Iago insinuates that Desdemona may be unfaithful. Hitherto all his efforts have been directed to rousing suspicion of Cassio [K].   166–7 *mock . . . feeds on* Jealousy is conceived of not as something arising from within man, but as a lurking monster from without, which seizes upon man (his meat) and plays with him as a cat plays with a mouse.   168 *his wronger* the wife who is betraying him.   170 *strongly* Q¹; Some editors read "fondly," an emendation of F¹ "soundly."   173 *fineless* boundless.

From jealousy!

OTH.   Why, why is this?
Think'st thou I'ld make a life of jealousy,
To follow still the changes of the moon
With fresh suspicions? No! To be once in doubt
Is once to be resolv'd. Exchange me for a goat   180
When I shall turn the business of my soul
To such exsufflicate and blown surmises,
Matching thy inference. 'Tis not to make me jealous
To say my wife is fair, feeds well, loves company,
Is free of speech, sings, plays, and dances well.   185
Where virtue is, these are more virtuous.
Nor from mine own weak merits will I draw
The smallest fear or doubt of her revolt,
For she had eyes, and chose me. No Iago;
I'll see before I doubt; when I doubt, prove;   190
And on the proof there is no more but this —
Away at once with love or jealousy!

IAGO.   I am glad of it; for now I shall have reason
To show the love and duty that I bear you
With franker spirit. Therefore, as I am bound,   195
Receive it from me. I speak not yet of proof.
Look to your wife; observe her well with Cassio;
Wear your eye thus, not jealous nor secure.
I would not have your free and noble nature,
Out of self-bounty, be abus'd. Look to't.   200
I know our country disposition well:
In Venice they do let heaven see the pranks
They dare not show their husbands; their best conscience

---

178 *still* ever, always.   180 *to be resolv'd* to have doubt cleared up.   182 *exsuf-*
flicate insubstantial, blown up with air. *blown* (a) blown up (b) flyblown, odious.
183 *Matching thy inference* in accordance with your description of the suspicions
of a jealous man [K].   186 *Where virtue . . . more virtuous* when a woman is
virtuous, these things merely add to her excellence. "Virtue," besides its specific
meaning, often signifies "excellence" of any kind [K].   187 *weak merits* unattrac-
tive physical features.   188 *revolt* unfaithfulness.   190 *prove* put the matter to a
test.   191 *on the proof* as a result of the test.   195 *franker* more open.   198
jealous suspicious. *secure* blindly confident.   199 *free* open and generous.   200

Is not to leave't undone, but keep't unknown.

OTH.   Dost thou say so?   205

IAGO.   She did deceive her father, marrying you;
And when she seem'd to shake and fear your looks,
She lov'd them most.

OTH.   And so she did.

IAGO.   Why, go to then!
She that, so young, could give out such a seeming
To seel her father's eyes up close as oak —   210
He thought 'twas witchcraft — but I am much to blame.
I humbly do beseech you of your pardon
For too much loving you.

OTH.   I am bound to thee for ever.

IAGO.   I see this hath a little dash'd your spirits.

OTH.   Not a jot, not a jot.

IAGO.   I' faith, I fear it has.   215
I hope you will consider what is spoke
Comes from my love. But I do see y'are mov'd.
I am to pray you not to strain my speech
To grosser issues nor to larger reach
Than to suspicion.   220

OTH.   I will not.

IAGO.   Should you do so, my lord,
My speech should fall into such vile success
As my thoughts aim not at. Cassio's my worthy friend —
My lord, I see y'are mov'd.

---

self-bounty innate goodness. abus'd deceived, tricked. 201 I know . . . well
An insidious suggestion, as coming from one who is known to be uncommonly ob-
servant (cf. lines 259–60) and is regarded by all as "honest" [K]. Iago plays on the
fact that Othello is an alien in Venice, unfamiliar with its customs. 202–3 In
Venice . . . their husbands Historically, Venice was, in fact, famous for its
courtesans. 206–8 She did deceive . . . most Here and in his next speech Iago
recalls to Othello's mind Brabantio's ominous words (I.III.292–3) [K]. 210 seel
sew up (as in falconry). as oak as the grain of oak. 219 grosser issues
greater consequences. 222 fall into such vile success have such an odious result.

OTH.	No, not much mov'd.
	I do not think but Desdemona's honest. 225
IAGO.	Long live she so! and long live you to think so!
OTH.	And yet, how nature erring from itself —
IAGO.	Ay, there's the point! as (to be bold with you)
	Not to affect many proposed matches
	Of her own clime, complexion, and degree, 230
	Whereto we see in all things nature tends —
	Foh! one may smell in such a will most rank,
	Foul disproportion, thoughts unnatural —
	But pardon me — I do not in position
	Distinctly speak of her; though I may fear 235
	Her will, recoiling to her better judgment,
	May fall to match you with her country forms,
	And happily repent.
OTH.	Farewell, farewell!
	If more thou dost perceive, let me know more.
	Set on thy wife to observe. Leave me, Iago. 240
IAGO.	My lord, I take my leave. [Going.]
OTH.	Why did I marry? This honest creature doubtless
	Sees and knows more, much more, than he unfolds.
IAGO.	[returns] My lord, I would I might entreat your Honour
	To scan this thing no further. Leave it to time. 245
	Though it be fit that Cassio have his place,

225 *honest* chaste. 229 *affect* care for. Othello, in reflecting that nature may prove false to itself, is thinking of the possibility that Desdemona has sinned with Cassio. Iago instantly gives the remark a sinister twist. Desdemona's nature, he argues, has already "erred from itself," for it was abnormal for a woman like her to reject all the suitors of her own race and age and fall in love with a man like Othello. His argument is based on the general principle that "like will to like" [K]. 230 *clime* country. *complexion* (a) colour (b) temperament (literally, the peculiar combination of humours in the body). *degree* social rank. 232 *will* carnal desire. 233 *disproportion* abnormality. 234-5 *I do not . . . of her* I do not mean to lay down a proposition that applies to her in particular. Iago suggests, insidiously, that Desdemona may possibly be an exception to the general rule [K]. 236 *recoiling* reverting. 237 *fall to match you* chance to compare you. *her country forms* the physical appearances, forms of beauty, of her own country, Venice. 238 *And happily* and so, perhaps. The argument is that, if Desdemona's love for Othello was a mere caprice of passion, her nature may recover its balance, and she may come to dislike him [K]. She will compare his blackness to

For sure he fills it up with great ability,
Yet, if you please to hold him off awhile,
You shall by that perceive him and his means.
Note if your lady strain his entertainment   250
With any strong or vehement importunity.
Much will be seen in that. In the mean time
Let me be thought too busy in my fears
(As worthy cause I have to fear I am)
And hold her free, I do beseech your Honour.   255

OTH.   Fear not my government.

IAGO.   I once more take my leave.   *Exit.*

OTH.   This fellow's of exceeding honesty,
And knows all qualities, with a learned spirit
Of human dealings. If I do prove her haggard,   260
Though that her jesses were my dear heartstrings,
I'ld whistle her off and let her down the wind
To prey at fortune. Haply, for I am black
And have not those soft parts of conversation
That chamberers have, or for I am declin'd   265
Into the vale of years (yet that's not much),
She's gone. I am abus'd, and my relief
Must be to loathe her. O curse of marriage,
That we can call these delicate creatures ours,
And not their appetites! I had rather be a toad   270
And live upon the vapour of a dungeon

the handsome features of her own countrymen.   245 *scan* examine closely.   249
his means the means he uses to procure reinstatement [K].   250 *strain* press, urge.
his entertainment that he be entertained, received back into favour.   253 *too
busy* too much of a busybody.   255 *hold her free* consider her innocent.   256
government self-control.   259 *qualities* human natures.   259-60 *learned spirit
. . . dealings* mind experienced in the way in which people act in their dealings
with each other [K].   260 *haggard* wild, improperly trained, unfaithful. A "haggard" was a wild female hawk.   261 *jesses* straps, usually of leather, by which a
falcon's legs were attached to the leash.   *heartstrings* certain tendons or nerves
which, according to old notions of anatomy, were attached to the heart and supported it in place.   262 *whistle her off* the falconer's signal of dismissal or rejec-
tion [K].   262-3 *let her down . . . prey at fortune* let her fly away, whithersoever
chance may carry her; let her shift for herself and take such prey as fortune may
afford [K].   263 *Haply, for* perhaps because.   265 *chamberers* wanton gallants.
for because.   *declin'd . . . years* past the meridian of life [K].   267 *abus'd* deceived.

Than keep a corner in the thing I love
For others' uses. Yet 'tis the plague of great ones;
Prerogativ'd are they less than the base.
'Tis destiny unshunnable, like death. 275
Even then this forked plague is fated to us
When we do quicken. Desdemona comes.

Enter Desdemona *and* Emilia.

If she be false, O, then heaven mocks itself!
I'll not believe't.

DES. How now, my dear Othello?
Your dinner, and the generous islanders 280
By you invited, do attend your presence.

OTH. I am to blame.

DES. Why do you speak so faintly?
Are you not well?

OTH. I have a pain upon my forehead, here.

DES. Faith, that's with watching; 'twill away again. 285
Let me but bind it hard, within this hour
It will be well.

OTH. Your napkin is too little.

[*He puts the handkerchief from him,
and she drops it.*]

Let it alone. Come, I'll go in with you.

DES. I am very sorry that you are not well.

Exeunt Othello *and* Desdemona.

EMIL. I am glad I have found this napkin. 290

274 *Prerogativ'd* exempt by privilege (from this curse of unfaithfulness in marriage) [K]. The implication is that greatness in rank provides no exemption from
cuckoldry, but it is difficult to determine precisely Othello's meaning here. *base*
lowly (in social position). 276 *forked plague* plague of horns. The husband of
an unfaithful wife was said to have horns grow upon his forehead [K]. 277
quicken are born. 278-9 *If she be false . . . believe't* The sight of Desdemona
immediately brings Othello back from the condition to which Iago has reduced
him. Othello's fall is not an easy one, and with this appearance of Desdemona, the

This was her first remembrance from the Moor.
My wayward husband hath a hundred times
Woo'd me to steal it; but she so loves the token
(For he conjur'd her she should ever keep it)
That she reserves it evermore about her   295
To kiss and talk to. I'll have the work ta'en out
And give't Iago.
What he will do with it heaven knows, not I;
I nothing but to please his fantasy.

Enter Iago.

IAGO.   How now? What do you here alone?   300

EMIL.   Do not you chide; I have a thing for you.

IAGO.   A thing for me? It is a common thing —

EMIL.   Ha?

IAGO.   To have a foolish wife.

EMIL.   O, is that all? What will you give me now   305
      For that same handkerchief?

IAGO.   What handkerchief?

EMIL.   What handkerchief?
      Why, that the Moor first gave to Desdemona;
      That which so often you did bid me steal.

IAGO.   Hast stol'n it from her?   310

EMIL.   No, faith; she let it drop by negligence,
      And to th' advantage, I, being here, took't up.
      Look, here it is.

IAGO.   A good wench! Give it me.

EMIL.   What will you do with't, that you have been so earnest

---

struggle for his soul is resumed.   280 *generous* noble.   282 *to blame* at fault (for
keeping them waiting).   284 *upon my forehead* An allusion to the sprouting horns
of the cuckold. Desdemona does not understand.   285 *watching* loss of sleep.
287 *napkin* handkerchief.   291 *remembrance* keepsake.   292 *wayward* capricious.
294 *conjur'd her* made her swear.   296 *work* embroidery. *ta'en out* copied.   299
fantasy whim.   301 *thing* slang for sex organ.   302 *common* open to all. Iago is
calling his wife a whore.   304 *To have . . . wife* Emilia's "Ha" of understanding
causes Iago to change the tenour of his remark.   312 *to th' advantage* opportunely.

To have me filch it?

IAGO. <div style="text-align:center;">Why, what's that to you?</div> 315

[*Snatches it.*]

EMIL. If it be not for some purpose of import,
Give't me again. Poor lady, she'll run mad
When she shall lack it.

IAGO. Be not you acknown on't; I have use for it.
Go, leave me.   *Exit* Emilia. 320
I will in Cassio's lodging lose this napkin
And let him find it. Trifles light as air
Are to the jealous confirmations strong
As proofs of holy writ. This may do something.
The Moor already changes with my poison.   325
Dangerous conceits are in their natures poisons
Which at the first are scarce found to distaste,
But with a little act upon the blood
Burn like the mines of sulphur.

Enter Othello.

I did say so.
Look where he comes! Not poppy nor mandragora, 330
Nor all the drowsy syrups of the world,
Shall ever medicine thee to that sweet sleep
Which thou ow'dst yesterday.

OTH. Ha! ha! false to me?

IAGO. Why, how now, General? No more of that!

OTH. Avaunt! be gone! Thou hast set me on the rack. 335

---

316 *import* importance.   318 *lack* miss.   319 *Be not you acknown on't* don't acknowledge that you know anything about it.   325 *changes with* is affected by.
326 *conceits* conceptions, imaginings.   327 *distaste* taste bad.   328 *with a little
. . . blood* after a little action upon the blood.   329 *mines of sulphur* the sulphur mines on the Æolian islands between Sicily and Italy which, according to
Pliny's NATURAL HISTORY (XXXV, 15, 50, 174) caused those islands to be perpetually
aflame.   330 *poppy* opium.   *mandragora* mandrake, used in sleeping potions.
331 *drowsy syrups* sleeping potions.   333 *ow'dst* didst possess.   *Ha! ha! false to
me* Othello speaks to himself, not noticing the presence of Iago [K]. In the speeches
which follow Othello reveals an ever-increasing mental confusion; his reason is
collapsing.   336 *'tis better . . . abus'd* it is better to be the unknowing victim of

I swear 'tis better to be much abus'd
Than but to know't a little.

IAGO.   How now, my lord?

OTH.   What sense had I of her stol'n hours of lust?
I saw't not, thought it not, it harm'd not me.
I slept the next night well, fed well, was free and merry;   340
I found not Cassio's kisses on her lips.
He that is robb'd, not wanting what is stol'n.
Let him not know't, and he's not robb'd at all.

IAGO.   I am sorry to hear this.

OTH.   I had been happy if the general camp,   345
Pioners and all, had tasted her sweet body,
So I had nothing known. O, now for ever
Farewell the tranquil mind! farewell content!
Farewell the plumed troop, and the big wars
That make ambition virtue! O, farewell!   350
Farewell the neighing steed and the shrill trump,
The spirit-stirring drum, th' ear-piercing fife,
The royal banner, and all quality,
Pride, pomp, and circumstance of glorious war!
And O ye mortal engines whose rude throats   355
Th' immortal Jove's dread clamours counterfeit,
Farewell! Othello's occupation's gone!

IAGO.   Is't possible, my lord?

OTH.   Villain, be sure thou prove my love a whore!
Be sure of it; give me the ocular proof;   360
Or, by the worth of mine eternal soul,

deception.   338 *sense* feeling. By this time Othello has come to accept Iago's
slander of Desdemona without question.   340 *fed well* F¹; Q¹, κ omit, thus making
the line more metrical, but Alexandrines are common in Shakespeare.   342 *wanting* missing.   346 *Pioners* sappers, diggers of trenches, soldiers of the lowest rank.
347 *So* if only.   350 *make ambition virtue* ambition, which is usually reprehensi-
ble, is made justifiable and even meritorious by the splendour of warfare.   353
quality military rank.   354 *circumstance* splendour, pageantry.   357 *Othello's
occupation's gone* He can no longer be a soldier because, as a cuckold, his honour
has been forfeited.   358 *Is't possible* that you should be so beside yourself [κ].
361 *mine* F¹; Q¹, κ: "man's."

Thou hadst been better have been born a dog
Than answer my wak'd wrath!

IAGO.   Is't come to this?

OTH.   Make me to see't; or at the least so prove it
That the probation bear no hinge nor loop   365
To hang a doubt on — or woe upon thy life!

IAGO.   My noble lord —

OTH.   If thou dost slander her and torture me,
Never pray more; abandon all remorse;
On horror's head horrors accumulate;   370
Do deeds to make heaven weep, all earth amaz'd;
For nothing canst thou to damnation add
Greater than that.

IAGO.   O grace! O heaven forgive me!
Are you a man? Have you a soul or sense? —
God b' wi' you! take mine office. O wretched fool,   375
That liv'st to make thine honesty a vice!
O monstrous world! Take note, take note, O world,
To be direct and honest is not safe.
I thank you for this profit; and from hence
I'll love no friend, sith love breeds such offence.   380

OTH.   Nay, stay. Thou shouldst be honest.

IAGO.   I should be wise; for honesty 's a fool
And loses that it works for.

OTH.   By the world,
I think my wife be <u>honest</u>, and think she is not;
I think that thou art just, and think thou art not.   385
I'll have some proof. Her name, that was as fresh

363 *answer* be exposed to, meet.   365 *probation* proof.   369 *remorse* compassion
or humane feeling—not remorse of conscience [K].   371 *all earth amaz'd* to make
all mankind paralyzed with horror [K].   376 *vice* fault.   379 *profit* lesson. *hence*
this time forth.   380 *sith love . . . offence* since I find that love for a friend
does me such injury, by making my friend distrust me [K].   381 *shouldst be* ought
to be, probably are.   383 *that it works for* trust.   384 *honest* chaste.   385 *just*
honest, upright.   386 *fresh* stainless.   387 *Dian's visage* the white face of Diana,
goddess of the moon (hence white) and of chastity.   392 *put* suggested this doubt.

As Dian's visage, is now begrim'd and black
As mine own face. If there be cords, or knives,
Poison, or fire, or suffocating streams,
I'll not endure it. Would I were satisfied!   390

IAGO.   I see, sir, you are eaten up with passion.
I do repent me that I put it to you.
You would be satisfied?

OTH.   Would? Nay, I will.

IAGO.   And may. But how? how satisfied, my lord?
Would you, the supervisor, grossly gape on?   395
Behold her topp'd?

OTH.   Death and damnation! O!

IAGO.   It were a tedious difficulty, I think,
To bring them to that prospect. Damn them then,
If ever mortal eyes do see them bolster
More than their own! What then? How then?   400
What shall I say? Where's satisfaction?
It is impossible you should see this,
Were they as prime as goats, as hot as monkeys,
As salt as wolves in pride, and fools as gross
As ignorance made drunk. But yet, I say,   405
If imputation and strong circumstances
Which lead directly to the door of truth
Will give you satisfaction, you may have't.

OTH.   Give me a living reason she's disloyal.

IAGO.   I do not like the office.   410
But sith I am enter'd in this cause so far,
Prick'd to't by foolish honesty and love,
I will go on. I lay with Cassio lately,

---

395 *supervisor* eyewitness. Iago now becomes more brutal and direct, goading
Othello to madness with visual details.   395 *gape* stare open-mouthed.   398
bring them to that prospect cause them to present such a view.   399 *bolster* go to
bed together.   403 *prime* lecherous. *goats* traditional symbols of lechery. *monkeys* also proverbially lustful animals.   404 *salt* lustful. *pride* heat.   406 *imputation . . . circumstances* such proofs of guilt as come from strong circumstantial
evidence [K].   409 *living* based on experience rather than conjecture.   411 *sith*
since.   412 *Prick'd* urged, spurred on.   413 *lay* slept.

And being troubled with a raging tooth,
I could not sleep. 415
There are a kind of men so loose of soul
That in their sleeps will mutter their affairs.
One of this kind is Cassio.
In sleep I heard him say, "Sweet Desdemona,
Let us be wary, let us hide our loves!" 420
And then, sir, would he gripe and wring my hand,
Cry "O sweet creature!" and then kiss me hard,
As if he pluck'd up kisses by the roots
That grew upon my lips; then laid his leg
Over my thigh, and sigh'd, and kiss'd, and then 425
Cried "Cursed fate that gave thee to the Moor!"

OTH. O monstrous! monstrous!

IAGO. Nay, this was but his dream.

OTH. But this denoted a foregone conclusion.
'Tis a shrewd doubt, though it be but a dream.

IAGO. And this may help to thicken other proofs 430
That do demonstrate thinly.

OTH. I'll tear her all to pieces!

IAGO. Nay, but be wise. Yet we see nothing done;
She may be honest yet. Tell me but this —
Have you not sometimes seen a handkerchief
Spotted with strawberries in your wife's hand? 435

OTH. I gave her such a one; 'twas my first gift.

IAGO. I know not that; but such a handkerchief
(I am sure it was your wife's) did I to-day

---

421 *gripe* grip. 428 *But this . . . conclusion* although what he said and did was
in a dream, it nevertheless pointed definitely to something that he had actually
experienced before [K]. 429 *shrewd doubt* painfully suspicious thing. Q¹, followed by some editors, gives this line to Iago; F¹ is followed here. 430 *thicken*
add to. 442 *the slave* Cassio. 445 *fond* foolish. 447 *the hollow hell* Vengeance
is conceived as dwelling in the nethermost abyss—the infernal regions [K] (F¹; Q¹:
"thy hollow cell"). 448 *hearted throne* throne in my heart. 449 *fraught* freight,
burden. 450 *aspics'* asps'. 452 *Your mind . . . change* Iago makes this insidious
suggestion in order to win from Othello some definite expression of his purpose of
vengeance. By suggesting that the Moor's mind may change he takes the best means

        See Cassio wipe his beard with.

OTH.   If't be that —

IAGO.   If it be that, or any that was hers,   440
          It speaks against her, with the other proofs.

OTH.   O, that the slave had forty thousand lives!
          One is too poor, too weak for my revenge.
          Now do I see 'tis true. Look here, Iago:
          All my fond love thus do I blow to heaven.   445
          'Tis gone.
          Arise, black vengeance, from the hollow hell!
          Yield up, O love, thy crown and hearted throne
          To tyrannous hate! Swell, bosom, with thy fraught,
          For 'tis of aspics' tongues!

IAGO.   Yet be content.   450

OTH.   O, blood, blood, blood!

IAGO.   Patience, I say. Your mind perhaps may change.

OTH.   Never, Iago. Like to the Pontic sea,
          Whose icy current and compulsive course
          Ne'er feels retiring ebb, but keeps due on   455
          To the Propontic and the Hellespont;
          Even so my bloody thoughts, with violent pace,
          Shall ne'er look back, ne'er ebb to humble love,
          Till that a capable and wide revenge
          Swallow them up. (*He kneels.*) Now, by yond marble
              heaven,   460
          In the due reverence of a sacred vow
          I here engage my words.

[handwritten margin note: Take out / Sword (cross) / make oath]

---

for confirming Othello's resolution. His success is shown by the fact that he receives before the end of the scene distinct orders to put Cassio out of the way [K].
453 *Pontic sea* Black Sea.   454 *compulsive* all-compelling, irresistible.   455 *feels* Q²; F¹: "keepes"; omitted in Q¹.   456 *Propontic* Sea of Marmora. *Hellespont* the Bosporus. In Philemon Holland's translation of Pliny's NATURAL HISTORY (1601), Shakespeare may have read that "The sea Pontus euermore floweth and runneth out into Propontis, but the sea neuer retireth backe again within Pontus."   459 *capable* capacious, all-embracing.   460 *marble* The adjective "marble" was an established epithet for the sky when Shakespeare wrote [K]. Precisely what it meant is not clear.   462 *engage* pledge.

IAGO.   Do not rise yet.   Iago *kneels.*
           Witness, you ever-burning lights above,
           You elements that clip us round about,
           Witness that here Iago doth give up   465
           The execution of his wit, hands, heart
           To wrong'd Othello's service! Let him command,
           And to obey shall be in me remorse,
           What bloody business ever.   [*They rise.*]

OTH.   I greet thy love,
           Not with vain thanks but with acceptance bounteous,   470
           And will upon the instant put thee to't.
           Within these three days let me hear thee say
           That Cassio's not alive.

IAGO.   My friend is dead; 'tis done at your request.
           But let her live.

OTH.   Damn her, lewd minx! O, damn her!   475
           Come, go with me apart. I will withdraw
           To furnish me with some swift means of death
           For the fair devil. Now art thou my lieutenant.

IAGO.   I am your own for ever.   *Exeunt.*

◇◇◇◇◇◇◇◇◇◇◇◇◇◇◇◇◇

SCENE IV. [*Cyprus. Before the Castle.*]

Enter Desdemona, Emilia, *and* Clown.

DES.   Do you know, sirrah, where Lieutenant Cassio lies?

CLOWN.   I dare not say he lies anywhere.

---

464 *clip* embrace.   466 *execution of his wit* all that his intellect can do [K].   468
to obey . . . remorse however bloody the work that Othello enjoins, I shall regard its performance not as cruelty but as pity. This may be taken merely as
strong hyperbole, or as indicating that Iago will regard the work as done out of
compassion for Othello's wrongs [K].   469 *greet* meet.   471 *to't* to the test.   479
I am your own for ever In this solemn ritual of kneeling and swearing Othello
and Iago are, in effect, symbolically joined. It is the seal of Othello's acceptance
of evil and total commitment to it.
     III.iv. 1 *lies* lodges. The clown takes the word in its other sense.   9–10 *lie*

DES.   Why, man?

CLOWN.   He's a soldier; and for one to say a soldier lies is stabbing.

DES.   Go to. Where lodges he?   5

CLOWN.   To tell you where he lodges is to tell you where I lie.

DES.   Can anything be made of this?

CLOWN.   I know not where he lodges; and for me to devise a
         lodging, and say he lies here or he lies there, were to lie
         in mine own throat.   10

DES.   Can you inquire him out, and be edified by report?

CLOWN.   I will catechize the world for him; that is, make ques-
         tions, and by them answer.

DES.   Seek him, bid him come hither. Tell him I have mov'd
         my lord on his behalf and hope all will be well.   15

CLOWN.   To do this is within the compass of man's wit, and there-
         fore I'll attempt the doing of it.   *Exit.*

DES.   Where should I lose that handkerchief, Emilia?

EMIL.   I know not, madam.

DES.   Believe me, I had rather have lost my purse   20
         Full of crusadoes; and but my noble Moor
         Is true of mind, and made of no such baseness
         As jealous creatures are, it were enough
         To put him to ill thinking.

EMIL.   Is he not jealous?

DES.   Who? he? I think the sun where he was born   25
         Drew all such humours from him.

---

in mine own throat tell a deep, deliberate lie—as contrasted with a casual misrepresentation or "white lie" [K].   11 *edified* instructed.   14 *mov'd* spoken to.
16 *compass* range.   21 *crusadoes* Portuguese gold coins bearing the stamp of a
cross. *but* but that.   24 *Is he not jealous* Emilia's general attitude is that all men
are jealous and that their difficulties must be put up with. This may in part
explain why she does not reveal the theft of the handkerchief. She must put up
with her "wayward" husband in spite of any misgivings about what he has asked
her to do.   26 *humours* whims.

Enter Othello.

EMIL.   Look where he comes.

DES.   I will not leave him now till Cassio
Be call'd to him. — How is't with you, my lord?

OTH.   Well, my good lady. [*Aside*] O, hardness to dissemble! —
How do you, Desdemona?

DES.   Well, my good lord.   30

OTH.   Give me your hand. This hand is moist, my lady.

DES.   It yet hath felt no age nor known no sorrow.

OTH.   This argues fruitfulness and liberal heart.
Hot, hot, and moist. This hand of yours requires
A sequester from liberty, fasting and prayer,   35
Much castigation, exercise devout;
For here's a young and sweating devil here
That commonly rebels. 'Tis a good hand,
A frank one.

DES.   You may, indeed, say so;
For 'twas that hand that gave away my heart.   40

OTH.   A liberal hand! The hearts of old gave hands;
But our new heraldry is hands, not hearts.

DES.   I cannot speak of this. Come now, your promise!

OTH.   What promise, chuck?

DES.   I have sent to bid Cassio come speak with you.   45

OTH.   I have a salt and sorry rheum offends me.
Lend me thy handkerchief.

---

31 *hand is moist* A hot moist palm was taken as an indication of a lustful temperament, just as a dry palm indicated sexual debility.   33 *liberal* free (with the
affections), wanton.   35 *sequester* retirement.   36 *castigation* austere self-disci-
pline.   37 *devil* the spirit of sensual desire [K].   38 *rebels* against virtuous self-
control [K].   39 *frank* Several meanings are possible: (a) candid, outspoken, which
reveals its owner's nature (b) generous. Desdemona takes it in the second sense.
41 *hearts . . . hands* love (hearts) in former times (old days) prescribed marriage
(hands).   42 *new heraldry . . . hearts* our new-fashioned symbolism (heraldry)
prescribes the joining of hands (marriage) without love (not hearts). It has been
suggested that the line is a reference to a new order of baronets created by King

DES.   Here, my lord.

OTH.   That which I gave you.

DES.   I have it not about me.

OTH.   Not?

DES.   No indeed, my lord.

OTH.   That is a fault.
That handkerchief   50
Did an Egyptian to my mother give.
She was a charmer, and could almost read
The thoughts of people. She told her, while she kept it,
'Twould make her amiable and subdue my father
Entirely to her love; but if she lost it   55
Or made a gift of it, my father's eye
Should hold her loathly, and his spirits should hunt
After new fancies. She, dying, gave it me,
And bid me, when my fate would have me wive,
To give it her. I did so; and take heed on't;   60
Make it a darling like your precious eye.
To lose't or give't away were such perdition
As nothing else could match.

DES.   Is't possible?

OTH.   'Tis true. There's magic in the web of it.
A sibyl that had numb'red in the world   65
The sun to course two hundred compasses,
In her prophetic fury sew'd the work;
The worms were hallowed that did breed the silk;
And it was dy'd in mummy which the skilful

James I in 1612, of which the heraldic badge was an addition of a hand gules to the coat of arms. If so, the line would constitute a later addition to Shakespeare's text, but the similarity may be entirely coincidental.   44 *chuck* chick (a term of affection).   46 *rheum* cold in the head.   *offends* troubles.   51 *an Egyptian* an Egyptian sorceress; a gypsy. The gypsies were thought to be of Egyptian origin [K]. 54 *amiable* desirable, lovable (much stronger than in our modern sense).   58 *fancies* loves.   62 *perdition* irrevocable loss (like the soul's damnation).   64 *web* weave. 65 *sibyl* prophetess.   66 *compasses* yearly circuits.   67 *fury* wild fit of inspiration. *work* embroidered pattern.   69 *mummy* liquid supposedly derived from embalmed human flesh, reputed to have great medicinal and magical properties.

        Conserv'd of maiden's hearts.

DES.   I' faith? Is't true?   70

OTH.   Most veritable. Therefore look to't well.

DES.   Then would to God that I had never seen't!

OTH.   Ha! Wherefore?

DES.   Why do you speak so startingly and rash?

OTH.   Is't lost? Is't gone? Speak, is it out o' th' way?   75

DES.   Heaven bless us!

OTH.   Say you?

DES.   It is not lost. But what an if it were?

OTH.   How?

DES.   I say it is not lost.

OTH.   Fetch't, let me see't!   80

DES.   Why, so I can, sir; but I will not now.
        This is a trick to put me from my suit.
        Pray you let Cassio be receiv'd again.

OTH.   Fetch me the handkerchief! My mind misgives.

DES.   Come, come!   85
        You'll never meet a more sufficient man.

OTH.   The handkerchief!

DES.   I pray talk me of Cassio.

OTH.   The handkerchief!

DES.   A man that all his time
        Hath founded his good fortunes on your love,
        Shar'd dangers with you —   90

---

70 *Conserv'd* prepared as a drug. *of* out of. 74 *startingly* disconnectedly, with fits and starts. *rash* hastily, urgently. 78 *It is not lost* Desdemona is startled (though not frightened), and she is unwilling to admit even to herself that the handkerchief is "lost": it is, she thinks, merely mislaid [K]. 86 *sufficient* able. 92 *to blame* blameworthy—for speaking so roughly to me. 95 *this* this trait— such violence on Othello's part [K]. 98 *'Tis not . . . a man* it does not take as much as a year or two for a man to reveal his true nature: he reveals it much

OTH.	The handkerchief!
DES.	In sooth, you are to blame.
OTH.	Away! *Exit.*
EMIL.	Is not this man jealous?
DES.	I ne'er saw this before.

DES. I ne'er saw this before.   95
Sure there's some wonder in this handkerchief.
I am most unhappy in the loss of it.

EMIL. 'Tis not a year or two shows us a man.
They are all but stomachs, and we all but food;
They eat us hungerly, and when they are full,   100
They belch us.

Enter Iago *and* Cassio.

Look you — Cassio and my husband!

IAGO. There is no other way; 'tis she must do't.
And lo the happiness! Go and importune her.

DES. How now, good Cassio? What's the news with you?

CAS. Madam, my former suit. I do beseech you   105
That by your virtuous means I may again
Exist, and be a member of his love
Whom I with all the office of my heart
Entirely honour. I would not be delay'd.
If my offence be of such mortal kind   110
That neither service past, nor present sorrows,
Nor purpos'd merit in futurity,
Can ransom me into his love again,
But to know so must be my benefit.
So shall I clothe me in a forc'd content,   115
And shut myself up in some other course,

sooner.   99 *stomachs* sexual appetites.   106 *virtuous means* powerful ability to help.   107 *be a member of* have a share in.   108 *office* devoted service.   112 *purpos'd merit in futurity* esteem (merit) I am determined to deserve in the future.   114 *But to know . . . benefit* I must regard it as a favour merely to know the worst. Anything is better than this uncertainty [K].   115 *clothe me . . . content* force myself to accept my situation.   116 *shut myself . . . course* confine myself to some humbler course of life [K].

To fortune's alms.

DES.   Alas, thrice-gentle Cassio!
My advocation is not now in tune.
My lord is not my lord; nor should I know him,
Were he in favour as in humour alter'd.   120
So help me every spirit sanctified
As I have spoken for you all my best
And stood within the blank of his displeasure
For my free speech! You must awhile be patient.
What I can do I will; and more I will   125
Than for myself I dare. Let that suffice you.

IAGO.   Is my lord angry?

EMIL.   He went hence but now,
And certainly in strange unquietness.

IAGO.   Can he be angry? I have seen the cannon
When it hath blown his ranks into the air   130
And, like the devil, from his very arm
Puff'd his own brother — and can he be angry?
Something of moment then. I will go meet him.
There's matter in't indeed if he be angry.

DES.   I prithee do so.   *Exit* [Iago].
                        Something sure of state,   135
Either from Venice or some unhatch'd practice
Made demonstrable here in Cyprus to him,
Hath puddled his clear spirit; and in such cases
Men's natures wrangle with inferior things,
Though great ones are their object. 'Tis even so.   140
For let our finger ache, and it endues
Our other, healthful, members even to that sense

---

117 *To fortune's alms* receiving from fortune whatever she can dole out to me.
118 *advocation* intercession, pleading. *in tune* well-received (like harmony).   120
favour features. *humour* disposition.   123 *within the blank of* in the range of;
the "blank" was the white spot at the center of a target.   135 *Something sure
of state* certainly some government business.   136 *unhatch'd practice* plot not
yet matured [K]. 137 *Made demonstrable* revealed.   138 *puddled* made muddy,
disturbed. *clear spirit* usual serenity of mind.   140 *object* target, real concern.
141 *endues* brings into accord.   144 *observancy* attention, devotion.   145 *fits the
bridal* is appropriate at the time of the wedding.   146 *unhandsome* improper,

Of pain. Nay, we must think men are not gods,
Nor of them look for such observancy
As fits the bridal. Beshrew me much, Emilia, 145
I was (unhandsome warrior as I am!)
Arraigning his unkindness with my soul;
But now I find I had suborn'd the witness,
And he's indicted falsely.

EMIL. Pray heaven it be state matters, as you think, 150
And no conception nor no jealous toy
Concerning you.

DES. Alas the day! I never gave him cause.

EMIL. But jealous souls will not be answer'd so.
They are not ever jealous for the cause, 155
But jealous for they are jealous. 'Tis a monster
Begot upon itself, born on itself.

DES. Heaven keep that monster from Othello's mind!

EMIL. Lady, amen.

DES. I will go seek him. Cassio, walk here about. 160
If I do find him fit, I'll move your suit
And seek to effect it to my uttermost.

CAS. I humbly thank your ladyship.

Exeunt Desdemona *and* Emilia.

Enter Bianca.

BIAN. Save you, friend Cassio!

CAS. What make you from home?
How is it with you, my most fair Bianca? 165

---

unfair. 147 *Arraigning . . . soul* accusing him of unkindness at my soul's tri-
bunal. The legal figure is carried out in what follows [K]. 148 *suborn'd the witness* induced him to swear falsely. The "witness" is Othello's harshness, which, she
says, she had induced to give false evidence against him—had wilfully misin-
terpreted [K]. It should be noted that Desdemona always takes upon herself the
blame for Othello's shortcomings. 151 *conception,* idea, notion. *jealous toy*
suspicious fancy. 161 *I'll move your suit* This shows how far Desdemona is from
suspecting that Cassio is involved, even when she has begun to entertain the idea
that Othello may be jealous [K].

I' faith, sweet love, I was coming to your house.

BIAN.   And I was going to your lodging, Cassio.
What, keep a week away? seven days and nights?
Eightscore eight hours? and lovers' absent hours,
More tedious than the dial eightscore times?   170
O weary reck'ning!

CAS.   Pardon me, Bianca.
I have this while with leaden thoughts been press'd;
But I shall in a more continuate time
Strike off this score of absence. Sweet Bianca,

            [*Gives her* Desdemona's *handkerchief.*]

Take me this work out.

BIAN.   O Cassio, whence came this?   175
This is some token from a newer friend.
To the felt absence now I feel a cause.
Is't come to this? Well, well.

CAS.   Go to, woman!
Throw your vile guesses in the devil's teeth,
From whence you have them. You are jealous now   180
That this is from some mistress, some remembrance.
No, by my faith, Bianca.

BIAN.   Why, whose is it?

CAS.   I know not, sweet. I found it in my chamber.
I like the work well. Ere it be demanded,
As like enough it will, I would have it copied.   185
Take it and do't, and leave me for this time.

BIAN.   Leave you? Wherefore?

CAS.   I do attend here on the General
And think it no addition, nor my wish,
To have him see me woman'd.

BIAN.   Why, I pray you?   190

---

170 *the dial* the whole round of the clock's hands [K].   172 *leaden* heavy.   *press'd*
oppressed.   173 *continuate* uninterrupted.   174 *Strike off this score* pay off this
debt. A "score" was a reckoning at a tavern.   175 *Take me this work out* copy
this embroidered pattern for me.   176 *friend* sweetheart.   188 *attend here on* wait

CAS.   Not that I love you not.

BIAN.   But that you do not love me!
        I pray you bring me on the way a little,
        And say if I shall see you soon at night.

CAS.   'Tis but a little way that I can bring you,
        For I attend here; but I'll see you soon.   195

BIAN.   'Tis very good. I must be circumstanc'd.   *Exeunt.*

---

here for.   189 *addition* credit to me.   190 *woman'd* accompanied by a woman.
Bianca's profession would be obvious enough from her dress and manner [K].
192 *bring . . . way* escort me.   194 *bring* accompany.   195 *attend* wait.   196
circumstanc'd satisfied with the necessities of the moment.

Act Four

<<<<<<<<<<<<<<<<<<<<<<<<<<<<<<>>>>>>>>>>>>>>>>>>>>>>>>>>>>>>>>

SCENE I. [*Cyprus. Before the Castle.*]

Enter Othello *and* Iago.

IAGO.   Will you think so?

OTH.   Think so, Iago?

IAGO.   What,
To kiss in private?

OTH.   An unauthoriz'd kiss.

IAGO.   Or to be naked with her friend in bed
An hour, or more, not meaning any harm?

OTH.   Naked in bed, Iago, and not mean harm?   5
It is hypocrisy against the devil.
They that mean virtuously, and yet do so,
The devil their virtue tempts, and they tempt heaven.

IAGO.   So they do nothing, 'tis a venial slip.
But if I give my wife a handkerchief —   10

OTH.   What then?

IAGO.   Why, then 'tis hers, my lord; and being hers,
She may, I think, bestow't on any man.

IV.I. 1 *Will you think so* Shakespeare telescopes time, indicating that Iago has worked further upon Othello since we last saw them, so that Othello is now reduced to complete credulity. 2 *unauthoriz'd* unwarrantable. 6 *hypocrisy against the devil* Hypocrisy against God is to act with an appearance of virtue but with evil intent. Hypocrisy against the devil, then, would be to act with an appearance of evil but without "meaning any harm" [K]. 8 *tempt heaven* make a wanton trial of heaven's power to keep them from sin [K]. 9 *So* provided that. *venial* excusable. 17 *They have . . . have it not* persons who are

92

OTH.	She is protectress of her honour too.	
	May she give that?	15

IAGO.	Her honour is an essence that's not seen;
	They have it very oft that have it not.
	But for the handkerchief —

OTH.   By heaven, I would most gladly have forgot it!
Thou said'st (O, it comes o'er my memory   20
As doth the raven o'er the infected house,
Boding to all!) he had my handkerchief.

IAGO.   Ay, what of that?

OTH.   That's not so good now.

IAGO.   What
If I had said I had seen him do you wrong?
Or heard him say — as knaves be such abroad   25
Who having, by their own importunate suit,
Or voluntary dotage of some mistress,
Convinced or supplied them, cannot choose
But they must blab —

OTH.   Hath he said anything?

IAGO.   He hath, my lord; but be you well assur'd,   30
No more than he'll unswear.

OTH.   What hath he said?

IAGO.   Faith, that he did — I know not what he did.

OTH.   What? what?

IAGO.   Lie —

OTH.   With her?

---

not honourable are often reputed to be honourable, and persons who are not so
reputed are often really honourable. Compare what Iago says of reputation
(II.III.251–2) [K].   **21** *raven . . . house* Ravens were believed to hover over houses
infected with the plague. They were traditional harbingers of death.   **22** *Boding*
ominous.   **25** *as . . . abroad* as there are such knaves at large.   **28** *Convinced*
overcome their reluctance (by importunate suit).   *supplied* satisfied (the voluntary
dotage of the mistress).   **28–9** *cannot choose . . . blab* are forced by inner necessity to blab (about their conquests).   **31** *unswear* deny on oath.

IAGO.   With her, on her; what you will.

OTH.   Lie with her? lie on her? — We say lie on her when they   35
           belie her. — Lie with her! Zounds, that's fulsome. —
           Handkerchief — confessions — handkerchief! — To con-
           fess, and be hang'd for his labour — first to be hang'd,
           and then to confess! I tremble at it. Nature would not
           invest herself in such shadowing passion without some   40
           instruction. It is not words that shakes me thus. — Pish!
           Noses, ears, and lips? Is't possible? — Confess? — hand-
           kerchief? — O devil!   *Falls in a trance.*

IAGO.   Work on,
           My medicine, work! Thus credulous fools are caught,   45
           And many worthy and chaste dames even thus,
           All guiltless, meet reproach. — What, ho! my lord!
           My lord, I say! Othello!

                         Enter Cassio.

                    How now, Cassio?

CAS.   What's the matter?

IAGO.   My lord is fall'n into an epilepsy.   50
           This is his second fit; he had one yesterday.

CAS.   Rub him about the temples.

IAGO.   No, forbear.
           The lethargy must have his quiet course.
           If not, he foams at mouth, and by-and-by
           Breaks out to savage madness. Look, he stirs.   55
           Do you withdraw yourself a little while.
           He will recover straight. When he is gone,

35–43 *Lie with . . . O devil* Shakespeare shifts into disjoined prose to indicate the
final collapse of Othello into incoherent madness.   37–8 *confess, and be hanged*
An old proverb. In practice the Elizabethan criminal was given a chance to confess before his hanging.   39–41 *Nature . . . instruction* my natural faculties would
not thus suddenly be overshadowed unless it were as a sign to teach me that what
I have heard is true [K].   52 *forbear* let him alone.   53 *lethargy* unconsciousness.
54 *by-and-by* immediately.   57 *straight* in a moment.   58 *on great occasion*
about important business.   60 *mock me* Any reference to his head makes Othello
think of the horns of a cuckold—"a horned man" [K].   64 *civil* among the citi-
zens.   66 *yok'd* attached to a cart like an ox; married.   67 *draw with you* (a)
be in the same situation (b) pull the cart as the ox, a horned beast, does.   68 *un-*

I would on great occasion speak with you.   *Exit* Cassio.
How is it, General? Have you not hurt your head?

OTH.   Dost thou mock me?

IAGO.   I mock you? No, by heaven.   60
Would you would bear your fortune like a man!

OTH.   A horned man's a monster and a beast.

IAGO.   There's many a beast then in a populous city,
And many a civil monster.

OTH.   Did he confess it?

IAGO.   Good sir, be a man.   65
Think every bearded fellow that's but yok'd
May draw with you. There's millions now alive
That nightly lie in those unproper beds
Which they dare swear peculiar. Your case is better.
O, 'tis the spite of hell, the fiend's arch-mock,   70
To lip a wanton in a secure couch,
And to suppose her chaste! No, let me know;
And knowing what I am, I know what she shall be.

OTH.   O, thou art wise! 'Tis certain.

IAGO.   Stand you awhile apart;
Confine yourself but in a patient list.   75
Whilst you were here, o'erwhelmed with your grief
(A passion most unsuiting such a man),
Cassio came hither. I shifted him away
And laid good 'scuse upon your ecstasy;
Bade him anon return, and here speak with me;   80
The which he promis'd. Do but encave yourself

---

proper not exclusively their own.   69 *peculiar* reserved for themselves.   *better*
because you know the truth [K].   71 *lip* kiss.   *secure* unsuspecting.   73 *And knowing . . . shall be* knowing my own essential nature as a man, I know also what
woman must be. In this is an indication of Iago's view of mankind as naturally
debased, cuckoldry the natural fate of the married man as treachery is the natural
characteristic of woman.   74 *O, thou . . . certain* Othello has come to see human-
ity through the eyes of Iago.   75 *in a patient list* within the bounds of patience.
77 *unsuiting* Q¹; F¹: "resulting"; CAPELL, K: "unfitting." There is little justification
for the emendation which merely provides a synonym for the Q¹ reading.   79
ecstasy fit of unconsciousness.   81 *encave* conceal.

And mark the fleers, the gibes, and notable scorns
That dwell in every region of his face;
For I will make him tell the tale anew —
Where, how, how oft, how long ago, and when   85
He hath, and is again to cope your wife.
I say, but mark his gesture. Marry, patience!
Or I shall say you are all in all in spleen,
And nothing of a man.

OTH.   Dost thou hear, Iago?
I will be found most cunning in my patience;   90
But (dost thou hear?) most bloody.

IAGO.   That's not amiss;
But yet keep time in all. Will you withdraw?

                                    [Othello *retires*.]

Now will I question Cassio of Bianca,
A housewife that by selling her desires
Buys herself bread and clothes. It is a creature   95
That dotes on Cassio, as 'tis the strumpet's plague
To beguile many and be beguil'd by one.
He, when he hears of her, cannot refrain
From the excess of laughter. Here he comes.

                          Enter Cassio.

As he shall smile, Othello shall go mad;   100
And his unbookish jealousy must construe
Poor Cassio's smiles, gestures, and light behaviour
Quite in the wrong. How do you now, Lieutenant?

CAS.   The worser that you give me the addition
Whose want even kills me.   105

---

82 *fleers* sneers.   86 *cope* encounter, close with.   87 *gesture* bearing, demeanour.
88 *in spleen* governed by impulses. Excited, irrational behaviour was traditionally
attributed to the action of the spleen.   92 *keep time* maintain control, act reason-
ably. The figure is from music.   94 *housewife* hussy.   101 *unbookish* ignorant.
102 *light* licentious.   104 *give . . . addition* call me lieutenant.   107 *power*
Q¹; F¹: "dowre" (dower) has much to recommend it, as Iago seems to be thinking in
terms of Cassio's marriage to Bianca.   108 *speed* succeed. *caitiff* wretch.   112
faintly half-heartedly, not really meaning it.   118 *Roman* proud fellow. The

IAGO.   Ply Desdemona well, and you are sure on't.
        Now, if this suit lay in Bianca's power,
        How quickly should you speed!

CAS.   Alas, poor caitiff!

OTH.   Look how he laughs already!

IAGO.   I never knew a woman love man so.   110

CAS.   Alas, poor rogue! I think, i' faith, she loves me.

OTH.   Now he denies it faintly, and laughs it out.

IAGO.   Do you hear, Cassio?

OTH.   Now he importunes him
        To tell it o'er. Go to! Well said, well said!

IAGO.   She gives it out that you shall marry her.   115
        Do you intend it?

CAS.   Ha, ha, ha!

OTH.   Do you triumph, Roman? Do you triumph?

CAS.   I marry her? What, a customer? Prithee bear some char-
        ity to my wit; do not think it so unwholesome. Ha, ha,   120
        ha!

OTH.   So, so, so, so! Laugh that wins!

IAGO.   Faith, the cry goes that you shall marry her.

CAS.   Prithee say true.

IAGO.   I am a very villain else.   125

OTH.   Have you scor'd me? Well.

CAS.   This is the monkey's own giving out. She is persuaded

word is suggested by "triumph" from a natural association of ideas [K]. 119 *customer* harlot. 119–20 *bear some . . . wit* have some belief in my intellect [K].
120 *unwholesome* diseased. 122 *Laugh that wins* let him laugh that wins (a common proverb). 123 *cry* rumour. 126 *scor'd me* There seem to be three possible
meanings: (a) "marked me (with infamy)"—as with lashes from a whip (b) "scored
me up," posted my name—as a cuckold (c) "added up my score," settled my account, summed me up. The third seems to be the best [K]. 127 *giving out* report.

I will marry her out of her own love and flattery, not out of my promise.

OTH.   Iago beckons me. Now he begins the story.   130

CAS.   She was here even now; she haunts me in every place. I was t'other day talking on the sea bank with certain Venetians, and thither comes the bauble, and, by this hand, she falls me thus about my neck —

OTH.   Crying "O dear Cassio!" as it were. His gesture imports 135 it.

CAS.   So hangs, and lolls, and weeps upon me; so hales and pulls me! Ha, ha, ha!

OTH.   Now he tells how she pluck'd him to my chamber. O, I see that nose of yours, but not that dog I shall throw't 140 to.

CAS.   Well, I must leave her company.

Enter Bianca.

IAGO.   Before me! Look where she comes.

CAS.   'Tis such another fitchew! marry, a perfum'd one. What do you mean by this haunting of me?   145

BIAN.   Let the devil and his dam haunt you! What did you mean by that same handkerchief you gave me even now? I was a fine fool to take it. I must take out the whole work? A likely piece of work that you should find it in your chamber and know not who left it there! This is 150 some minx's token, and I must take out the work? There! give it your hobby-horse. Wheresoever you had it, I'll take out no work on't.

CAS.   How now, my sweet Bianca? How now? how now?

OTH.   By heaven, that should be my handkerchief!   155

BIAN.   An you'll come to supper to-night, you may; an you will not, come when you are next prepar'd for.   *Exit.*

---

128 *flattery* self-deception.   133 *bauble* plaything, bit of frippery.   137 *hales* tugs at.   144 *fitchew* polecat, traditionally regarded as a lustful animal.   146 *dam* mother.   148 *take out* copy.   152 *hobby-horse* whore (easily mounted).   155

IAGO. After her, after her!

CAS. Faith, I must; she'll rail i' th' street else.

IAGO. Will you sup there?   160

CAS. Yes, I intend so.

IAGO. Well, I may chance to see you; for I would very fain speak with you.

CAS. Prithee come. Will you?

IAGO. Go to! say no more.   *Exit* Cassio. 165

OTH. [*comes forward*] How shall I murder him, Iago?

IAGO. Did you perceive how he laugh'd at his vice?

OTH. O Iago!

IAGO. And did you see the handkerchief?

OTH. Was that mine?   170

IAGO. Yours, by this hand! And to see how he prizes the foolish woman your wife! She gave it him, and he hath giv'n it his whore.

OTH. I would have him nine years a-killing! — A fine woman! a fair woman! a sweet woman!   175

IAGO. Nay, you must forget that.

OTH. Ay, let her rot, and perish, and be damn'd to-night; for she shall not live. No, my heart is turn'd to stone. I strike it, and it hurts my hand. O, the world hath not a sweeter creature! She might lie by an emperor's side and 180 command him tasks.

IAGO. Nay, that's not your way.

OTH. Hang her! I do but say what she is. So delicate with her needle! an admirable musician! O, she will sing the savageness out of a bear! Of so high and plenteous wit 185 and invention!

---

should be must be.   156 *An* if.   171 *prizes* values.   182 *your way* your usual manner of thinking and talking about her.

IAGO.   She's the worse for all this.

OTH.   O, a thousand thousand times! And then, of so gentle a
condition!

IAGO.   Ay, too gentle.   190

OTH.   Nay, that's certain. But yet the pity of it, Iago! O Iago,
the pity of it, Iago!

IAGO.   If you are so fond over her iniquity, give her patent to
offend; for if it touch not you, it comes near nobody.

OTH.   I will chop her into messes! Cuckold me!   195

IAGO.   O, 'tis foul in her.

OTH.   With mine officer!

IAGO.   That's fouler.

OTH.   Get me some poison, Iago, this night. I'll not expostulate
with her, lest her body and beauty unprovide my mind 200
again. This night, Iago!

IAGO.   Do it not with poison. Strangle her in her bed, even the
bed she hath contaminated.

OTH.   Good, good! The justice of it pleases. Very good!

IAGO.   And for Cassio, let me be his undertaker. You shall hear 205
more by midnight.

OTH.   Excellent good!   *A trumpet.*
        What trumpet is that same?

IAGO.   Something from Venice, sure.

        Enter Lodovico, Desdemona, *and* At-
tendants.

        'Tis Lodovico,
Come from the Duke; and see, your wife is with him.

188–9 *gentle a condition* high-born social status.   190 *gentle* yielding, to men.
193 *fond* foolish.   193 *patent* license.   194 *comes near* concerns, harms.   195
messes small bits of food.   199 *expostulate* reason, argue.   200 *unprovide my
mind* impair my resolution to act.   205 *be his undertaker* undertake to dispose
of him. Some modern readers need to be warned that "undertaker" in the sense
of "funeral undertaker" (contractor for funerals) is a sense unknown to Shake-

LOD.   God save you, worthy General!

OTH.   With all my heart, sir.

LOD.   The Duke and Senators of Venice greet you.   210

                              [*Gives him a letter.*]

OTH.   I kiss the instrument of their pleasures.

                        [*Opens the letter and reads.*]

DES.   And what's the news, good cousin Lodovico?

IAGO.   I am very glad to see you, signior. Welcome to Cyprus.

LOD.   I thank you. How does Lieutenant Cassio?

IAGO.   Lives, sir.

DES.   Cousin, there's fall'n between him and my lord   215
        An unkind breach; but you shall make all well.

OTH.   Are you sure of that?

DES.   My lord?

OTH.   [*reads*] "This fail you not to do, as you will — "

LOD.   He did not call; he's busy in the paper.   220
        Is there division 'twixt thy lord and Cassio?

DES.   A most unhappy one. I would do much
        T' atone them, for the love I bear to Cassio.

OTH.   Fire and brimstone!

DES.   My lord?

OTH.   Are you wise?

DES.   What, is he angry?

LOD.   May be the letter mov'd him;   225
        For, as I think, they do command him home,
        Deputing Cassio in his government.

---

speare's generation [κ].   211 *kiss* welcome, greet.   *instrument* the letter.   *pleasures* desires.   216 *shall* shall surely.   223 *atone* reconcile (literally, make one). 224 *Are you wise* Desdemona's continued expression of interest in Cassio seems to Othello like madness on her part, since he supposes that, being guilty, she must know that he suspects her and that her words will confirm his suspicion [κ]. 227 *government* position as governor.

DES.	By my troth, I am glad on't.
OTH.	Indeed?
DES.	My lord?
OTH.	I am glad to see you mad.
DES.	Why, sweet Othello!
OTH.	Devil! [*Strikes her.*] 230
DES.	I have not deserv'd this.
LOD.	My lord, this would not be believ'd in Venice,
	Though I should swear I saw't. 'Tis very much.
	Make her amends; she weeps.
OTH.	O devil, devil!
	If that the earth could teem with woman's tears, 235
	Each drop she falls would prove a crocodile.
	Out of my sight!
DES.	I will not stay to offend you. [*Going.*]
LOD.	Truly, an obedient lady.
	I do beseech your lordship call her back. 240
OTH.	Mistress!
DES.	My lord?
OTH.	What would you with her, sir?
LOD.	Who? I, my lord?
OTH.	Ay! You did wish that I would make her turn.
	Sir, she can turn, and turn, and yet go on,
	And turn again; and she can weep, sir, weep; 245
	And she's obedient; as you say, obedient,
	Very obedient. — Proceed you in your tears. —
	Concerning this, sir (O well-painted passion!),

---

229 *I am . . . mad* This line has long puzzled commentators and, in fact, defies rational explanation. There is some possibility of textual corruption.   235 *teem* become pregnant.   236 *falls* lets fall.   *crocodile* false tear. The crocodile, according to ancient accounts, wept for his victim before devouring him.   243 *turn* come back.   244 *can turn . . . go on* is skilful in advancing toward her evil purposes by devious ways [K]. "Turn" in this sense means "change."   246 *obedient* complaisant, yielding to whatever men ask of her.   248 *this* the letter.   254 *Goats*

I am commanded home. — Get you away;
I'll send for you anon. — Sir, I obey the mandate   250
And will return to Venice. — Hence, avaunt!

> [*Exit* Desdemona.]

Cassio shall have my place. And, sir, to-night
I do entreat that we may sup together.
You are welcome, sir, to Cyprus. — Goats and monkeys!

> *Exit.*

LOD.   Is this the noble Moor whom our full Senate   255
Call all in all sufficient? Is this the nature
Whom passion could not shake? whose solid virtue
The shot of accident nor dart of chance
Could neither graze nor pierce?

IAGO.   He is much chang'd.

LOD.   Are his wits safe? Is he not light of brain?   260

IAGO.   He's that he is. I may not breathe my censure.
What he might be — if what he might he is not —
I would to heaven he were!

LOD.   What, strike his wife?

IAGO.   Faith, that was not so well; yet would I knew
That stroke would prove the worst!

LOD.   Is it his use?   265
Or did the letters work upon his blood
And new-create this fault?

IAGO.   Alas, alas!
It is not honesty in me to speak
What I have seen and known. You shall observe him,
And his own courses will denote him so   270

---

and monkeys Both of these animals were types of lasciviousness [κ]   256 *all sufficient* the master of all situations.   257 *solid virtue* firm stability of character [κ].
259 *graze* by the shot.   *pierce* by the dart.   260 *safe* sound.   261 *that* that which.
breathe speak. *censure* judgment.   265 *use* custom.   266 *work upon his blood*
arouse his emotions.   267 *new-create* cause to be committed for the first time.
270 *courses* behaviour.

>That I may save my speech. Do but go after
>And mark how he continues.

LOD.   I am sorry that I am deceiv'd in him.   *Exeunt.*

❖❖❖❖❖❖❖❖❖❖❖❖❖❖

SCENE II. [*Cyprus. A room in the Castle.*]

Enter Othello *and* Emilia.

OTH.   You have seen nothing then?

EMIL.   Nor ever heard, nor ever did suspect.

OTH.   Yes, you have seen Cassio and she together.

EMIL.   But then I saw no harm, and then I heard
        Each syllable that breath made up between them.   5

OTH.   What, did they never whisper?

EMIL.   Never, my lord.

OTH.   Nor send you out o' th' way?

EMIL.   Never.

OTH.   To fetch her fan, her gloves, her mask, nor nothing?

EMIL.   Never, my lord.   10

OTH.   That's strange.

EMIL.   I durst, my lord, to wager she is honest,
        Lay down my soul at stake. If you think other,
        Remove your thought; it doth abuse your bosom.
        If any wretch have put this in your head,   15
        Let heaven requite it with the serpent's curse!
        For if she be not honest, chaste, and true,
        There's no man happy; the purest of their wives
        Is foul as slander.

IV.II. 3 *she* Common Elizabethan grammar [K].   9 *mask* worn often by Elizabethan ladies in public places.   14 *abuse* deceive.   16 *serpent's curse* the curse
pronounced upon the serpent in the Garden of Eden (GENESIS, III, 14).   18 *happy*
fortunate.   20 *bawd* brothel manager. Othello assumes that if Desdemona is
guilty Emilia must be her accomplice.   22 *closet lock and key* safekeeper of the

OTH.   Bid her come hither. Go.   *Exit* Emilia.
        She says enough; yet she's a simple bawd   20
        That cannot say as much. This is a subtle whore,
        A closet lock and key of villainous secrets;
        And yet she'll kneel and pray; I have seen her do't.

                    Enter Desdemona *and* Emilia.

DES.   My lord, what is your will?

OTH.   Pray, chuck, come hither.

DES.   What is your pleasure?

OTH.   Let me see your eyes.   25
        Look in my face.

DES.   What horrible fancy's this?

OTH.   [*to* Emilia] Some of your function, mistress.
        Leave procreants alone and shut the door;
        Cough or cry hem if anybody come.
        Your mystery, your mystery! Nay, dispatch!   30

                                Exit Emilia.

DES.   Upon my knees, what doth your speech import?
        I understand a fury in your words,
        But not the words.

OTH.   Why, what art thou?

DES.   Your wife, my lord; your true
        And loyal wife.

OTH.   Come, swear it, damn thyself;   35
        Lest, being like one of heaven, the devils themselves
        Should fear to seize thee. Therefore be double-damn'd —
        Swear thou art honest.

DES.   Heaven doth truly know it.

OTH.   Heaven truly knows that thou art false as hell.

---

storeroom (closet). Usually "closet" in Shakespeare refers to any small room, but
here it seems to have more specific application.   27 *your function* as bawd.
Othello pretends that Desdemona is a whore, Emilia her bawd, and he a client in
their brothel.   30 *mystery* trade. *dispatch* make haste.

DES.	To whom, my lord? With whom? How am I false?	40
OTH.	O, Desdemona! away! away! away!	
DES.	Alas the heavy day! Why do you weep?	
	Am I the motive of these tears, my lord?	
	If haply you my father do suspect	
	An instrument of this your calling back,	45
	Lay not your blame on me. If you have lost him,	
	Why, I have lost him too.	

OTH.   Had it pleas'd heaven

To try me with affliction, had they rain'd
All kinds of sores and shames on my bare head,
Steep'd me in poverty to the very lips,   50
Given to captivity me and my utmost hopes,
I should have found in some place of my soul
A drop of patience. But, alas, to make me
A fixed figure for the time of scorn
To point his slow unmoving finger at!   55
Yet could I bear that too; well, very well.
But there where I have garner'd up my heart,
Where either I must live or bear no life,
The fountain from the which my current runs
Or else dries up — to be discarded thence,   60
Or keep it as a cistern for foul toads
To knot and gender in — turn thy complexion there,
Patience, thou young and rose-lipp'd cherubin!
Ay, there look grim as hell!

DES.	I hope my noble lord esteems me honest.	65
OTH.	O, ay! as summer flies are in the shambles,	

---

42 *heavy* sorrowful.   43 *motive* moving cause.   44 *haply* perhaps.   47–8 *Had it pleas'd . . . affliction* Othello sees his supposed misfortunes as analogous to those of the suffering Job.   48 *they* the heavens.   53 *patience* ability to bear misfortunes with hope of ultimate good. The use of the word in this theological sense supports the Job analogy.   54 *time of scorn* scornful world.   55 *slow unmoving* The finger of the scornful world is slowly raised to the position of pointing; and then, after it has directed itself at its object, it becomes "unmoving"—never ceasing to point at the poor wretch who is set up as a "fixed figure" for contempt [K]. (Q¹; F¹: "slow, and mouing").   57 *garner'd up* stored the harvest of.   59 *fountain* spring, well-head.   61 *it* the fountain.   62 *knot and gender* be joined and mate with one another.   62–3 *turn thy . . . cherubin* at that point—when required to

That quicken even with blowing. O thou weed,
Who art so lovely fair, and smell'st so sweet,
That the sense aches at thee, would thou hadst ne'er
    been born!

DES.   Alas, what ignorant sin have I committed?   70

OTH.   Was this fair paper, this most goodly book,
Made to write "whore" upon? What committed?
Committed? O thou public commoner!
I should make very forges of my cheeks
That would to cinders burn up modesty,   75
Did I but speak thy deeds. What committed?
Heaven stops the nose at it, and the moon winks;
The bawdy wind, that kisses all it meets,
Is hush'd within the hollow mine of earth
And will not hear it. What committed?   80
Impudent strumpet!

DES.   By heaven, you do me wrong!

OTH.   Are not you a strumpet?

DES.   No, as I am a Christian!
If to preserve this vessel for my lord
From any other foul unlawful touch
Be not to be a strumpet, I am none.   85

OTH.   What, not a whore?

DES.   No, as I shall be sav'd!

OTH.   Is't possible?

DES.   O, heaven forgive us!

---

endure that—let the rosy cherub Patience change to grim and savage wrath [K].
64 *there* THEOBALD; F¹, Q¹: "here."   66 *summer flies* An image of horrible promis-
cuity [K].   *shambles* slaughterhouse.   67 *quicken . . . blowing* come to life like
maggots in flyblown meat [K].   70 *ignorant* unknown to me.   73 *commoner*
prostitute.   74 *make very forges of* burn up (with blushing).   77 *moon* symbol
of chastity.   *winks* closes her eyes so as not to see.   79 *mine* cave. The winds
were supposed to issue from the interior of the earth. So, when it was calm, they
had retired to their subterranean home [K].   83 *this vessel* myself. A Biblical figure. See for example, I PETER, III, 7; ROMANS, IX, 22 [K].   84 *other* F¹, Q²; Q¹:
"hated."

OTH.   I cry you mercy then.
I took you for that cunning whore of Venice
That married with Othello. — You, mistress,   90
That have the office opposite to Saint Peter
And keep the gate of hell!

                        Enter Emilia.

                        You, you, ay, you!
We have done our course. There's money for your pains.
I pray you turn the key, and keep our counsel.   *Exit.*

EMIL.   Alas, what does this gentleman conceive?   95
How do you, madam? How do you, my good lady?

DES.   Faith, half asleep.

EMIL.   Good madam, what's the matter with my lord?

DES.   With who?

EMIL.   Why, with my lord, madam.   100

DES.   Who is thy lord?

EMIL.   He that is yours, sweet lady.

DES.   I have none. Do not talk to me, Emilia.
I cannot weep; nor answer have I none
But what should go by water. Prithee to-night
Lay on my bed my wedding sheets, remember;   105
And call thy husband hither.

EMIL.   Here's a change indeed!

                                            Exit.

DES.   'Tis meet I should be us'd so, very meet.
How have I been behav'd, that he might stick
The small'st opinion on my least misuse?

---

88 *I cry you mercy* I beg your pardon. Othello returns to the "horrible fancy"
with which he had begun the interview. In summoning Emilia he pretends to take
her for a bawd [K].   92 *keep the gate of hell* cf. PROVERBS, VII, 27: "Her [the
harlot's] house is the way to hell, going down to the chambers of death" [K].   93
done our course completed our business.   94 *turn the key* to open the door.   *keep
our counsel* keep our interview a secret [K].   95 *conceive* imagine.   97 *half asleep*
Desdemona is stunned by Othello's violent language and tired out by the intensity
of her emotions [K]. She finds it difficult to believe that she has not been dreaming.

Enter Iago *and* Emilia.

IAGO.   What is your pleasure, madam? How is't with you?   110

DES.   I cannot tell. Those that do teach young babes
        Do it with gentle means and easy tasks.
        He might have chid me so; for, in good faith,
        I am a child to chiding.

IAGO.   What is the matter, lady?

EMIL.   Alas, Iago, my lord hath so bewhor'd her,   115
        Thrown such despite and heavy terms upon her
        As true hearts cannot bear.

DES.   Am I that name, Iago?

IAGO.   What name, fair lady?

DES.   Such as she says my lord did say I was.

EMIL.   He call'd her whore. A beggar in his drink   120
        Could not have laid such terms upon his callet.

IAGO.   Why did he so?

DES.   I do not know. I am sure I am none such.

IAGO.   Do not weep, do not weep. Alas the day!

EMIL.   Hath she forsook so many noble matches,   125
        Her father and her country, all her friends,
        To be call'd whore? Would it not make one weep?

DES.   It is my wretched fortune.

IAGO.   Beshrew him for't!
        How comes this trick upon him?

DES.   Nay, heaven doth know.

EMIL.   I will be hang'd if some eternal villain,   130

---

104 *go by water* be expressed in tears.   107 *meet* proper, fitting.   108 *been be-hav'd* behaved.   108-9 *might stick . . . least misuse* attach the slightest censure (opinion) to my smallest fault (misuse).   113 *chid* scolded.   114 *a child to chiding* like a child when I am scolded.   115 *bewhor'd her* treated her like a whore. To satisfy logical probability, we must assume that Emilia has been listening at the door.   116 *despite* abuse, contempt.   121 *callet* trull, vagabond harlot.   128 *Beshrew* curse.   129 *trick* freak behaviour.   130 *eternal* everlasting, unmitigated.

	Some busy and insinuating rogue,
	Some cogging, cozening slave, to get some office,
	Have not devis'd this slander. I'll be hang'd else.
IAGO.	Fie, there is no such man! It is impossible.
DES.	If any such there be, heaven pardon him!

IAGO. Fie, there is no such man! It is impossible.

DES. If any such there be, heaven pardon him!   135

EMIL. A halter pardon him! and hell gnaw his bones!
Why should he call her whore? Who keeps her company?
What place? what time? what form? what likelihood?
The Moor's abus'd by some most villainous knave,
Some base notorious knave, some scurvy fellow.   140
O heaven, that such companions thou'dst unfold,
And put in every honest hand a whip
To lash the rascals naked through the world
Even from the East to th' West!

IAGO.   Speak within door.

EMIL. O, fie upon them! Some such squire he was   145
That turn'd your wit the seamy side without
And made you to suspect me with the Moor.

IAGO. You are a fool. Go to.

DES.   O good Iago,
What shall I do to win my lord again?
Good friend, go to him; for, by this light of heaven,   150
I know not how I lost him. Here I kneel.
If e'er my will did trespass 'gainst his love,
Either in discourse of thought or actual deed,
Or that mine eyes, mine ears, or any sense
Delighted them in any other form,   155

---

131 *busy* prying.   132 *cogging, cozening* Both words mean "cheating."   *to get some office* Emilia has no suspicion that her description fits Iago. Her horrified surprise when his guilt is revealed (v.ii.140*ff.*) leaves no room for doubt that until that moment she had not suspected his villainy [κ]. There are nevertheless inconsistencies in Emilia's behaviour which no amount of logical analysis will explain. 134 *no such* none so bad.   136 *halter* hangman's noose.   138 *form* evidence. 139 *abus'd* deceived.   140 *notorious* notable.   *scurvy* vile.   141 *companions* knaves.   *unfold* reveal, expose.   144 *within door* not so loudly.   145 *squire* used contemptuously.   146 *seamy side without* wrong side out.   147 *suspect . . . Moor* Iago has apparently made Emilia aware of his suspicions of her. It is ironical that Iago should have given his wife the opportunity for denial whereas the more

Or that I do not yet, and ever did,
And ever will (though he do shake me off
To beggarly divorcement) love him dearly,
Comfort forswear me! Unkindness may do much;
And his unkindness may defeat my life, 160
But never taint my love. I cannot say "whore."
It doth abhor me now I speak the word;
To do the act that might th' addition earn
Not the world's mass of vanity could make me.

IAGO. I pray you be content. 'Tis but his humour. 165
The business of the state does him offence,
And he does chide with you.

DES. If 'twere no other —

IAGO. 'Tis but so, I warrant.

[*Trumpets within.*]

Hark how these instruments summon you to supper.
The messengers of Venice stay the meat. 170
Go in, and weep not. All things shall be well.

Exeunt Desdemona *and* Emilia.

Enter Roderigo.

How now, Roderigo?

ROD. I do not find that thou deal'st justly with me.

IAGO. What in the contrary?

ROD. Every day thou daff'st me with some device, Iago, and 175
rather, as it seems to me now, keep'st from me all con-

---

noble Othello should have been incapable of such action.   153 *discourse of thought*
process of thought (with no notion of speech).   159 *Comfort forswear me* may
all that sustains life and makes it happy forsake me as if by a solemn vow [K].
160 *defeat* destroy.   161 *never taint my love* In the unshakable love of Desdemona
for Othello in spite of what tortures she may suffer at his hands, some critics have
seen an analogy to Christ's love for mankind.   162 *abhor* disgust.   163 *addition*
title (of whore).   164 *world's mass of vanity* this whole world with all its vain
delights [K].   165 *humour* mood.   170 *messengers of Venice* Lodovico and his
associates. *stay the meat* are waiting for supper.   175 *daff'st me* put me off.
device trick.   176 *conveniency* opportunity (to court Desdemona).

veniency than suppliest me with the least advantage of
hope. I will indeed no longer endure it; nor am I yet
persuaded to put up in peace what already I have fool-
ishly suffer'd.   180

IAGO.   Will you hear me, Roderigo?

ROD.   Faith, I have heard too much; for your words and performance are no kin together.

IAGO.   You charge me most unjustly.

ROD.   With naught but truth. I have wasted myself out of 185
means. The jewels you have had from me to deliver to
Desdemona would half have corrupted a votarist. You
have told me she hath receiv'd them, and return'd me
expectations and comforts of sudden respect and ac-
quaintance; but I find none.   190

IAGO.   Well, go to; very well.

ROD.   Very well! go to! I cannot go to, man; nor 'tis not very
well. Nay, I think it is scurvy, and begin to find myself
fopp'd in it.

IAGO.   Very well.   195

ROD.   I tell you 'tis not very well. I will make myself known
to Desdemona. If she will return me my jewels, I will
give over my suit and repent my unlawful solicitation.
If not, assure yourself I will seek satisfaction of you.

IAGO.   You have said now.   200

ROD.   Ay, and said nothing but what I protest intendment of
doing.

177–8 *advantage of hope* advantage that may further my hopes [K].   179 *put up
in peace* endure without resentment [K].   180 *suffer'd* permitted to occur.   187
votarist nun.   189 *comforts* comforting reports.   *sudden* immediate.   *respect* consideration (on Desdemona's part).   189–90 *acquaintance* meeting (with her) (F¹,
Q²; Q¹: "acquittance"—release from debt).   191 *go to* enough; say no more. Iago
speaks as if Roderigo's complaints were the last straw [K].   194 *fopp'd* made a fool
of.   196 *make myself known* Roderigo means simply that he will have a personal
explanation with Desdemona. So far Iago has managed to prevent an interview
(cf. line 189–90).   There is certainly no reference to Roderigo's being disguised [K].
198 *give over* abandon.   199 *seek satisfaction* demand repayment (or challenge to

IAGO.   Why, now I see there's mettle in thee; and even from
this instant do build on thee a better opinion than ever
before. Give me thy hand, Roderigo. Thou hast taken 205
against me a most just exception; but yet I protest I have
dealt most directly in thy affair.

ROD.   It hath not appear'd.

IAGO.   I grant indeed it hath not appear'd; and your suspicion 210
is not without wit and judgment. But, Roderigo, if thou
hast that in thee indeed which I have greater reason to
believe now than ever (I mean purpose, courage, and
valour), this night show it. If thou the next night following enjoy not Desdemona, take me from this world with 215
treachery and devise engines for my life.

ROD.   Well, what is it? Is it within reason and compass?

IAGO.   Sir, there is especial commission come from Venice to
depute Cassio in Othello's place.

ROD.   Is that true? Why, then Othello and Desdemona return 220
again to Venice.

IAGO.   O, no. He goes into Mauritania and takes away with him
the fair Desdemona, unless his abode be linger'd here by
some accident; wherein none can be so determinate as
the removing of Cassio.   225

ROD.   How do you mean removing of him?

IAGO: Why, by making him uncapable of Othello's place —
knocking out his brains.

ROD.   And that you would have me to do?

IAGO.   Ay, if you dare do yourself a profit and a right. He sups 230

---

a duel).   200 *You have said now* Iago pretends to be admiring Roderigo's spirit.
A modern equivalent might be "Now you're talking."   201 *protest* proclaim.
intendment intention.   203 *mettle* spirit and courage.   206 *just exception* fair
objection or criticism.   207 *directly* fairly, straightforwardly.   216 *engines for*
plots against.   217 *within reason and compass* within reasonable compass—within
the reasonable limits of accomplishment [K].   222 *Mauritania* the supposed home
of the Moors in Northwest Africa. The name is Roman.   223 *abode* stay. *linger'd*
lengthened.   224 *wherein none . . . determinate* and no occurrence can be so
decisive in lengthening his stay [K].   227 *uncapable of* unable to succeed to.
place position (as governor).

to-night with a harlotry, and thither will I go to him.
He knows not yet of his honourable fortune. If you will
watch his going thence, which I will fashion to fall out
between twelve and one, you may take him at your pleasure. I will be near to second your attempt, and he shall   235
fall between us. Come, stand not amaz'd at it, but go
along with me. I will show you such a necessity in his
death that you shall think yourself bound to put it on
him. It is now high supper time, and the night grows to
waste. About it!   240

ROD.   I will hear further reason for this.

IAGO.   And you shall be satisfied.   *Exeunt.*

◇◇◇◇◇◇◇◇◇◇◇◇◇◇◇

SCENE III.
[*Cyprus. Another room in the Castle.*]

Enter Othello, Lodovico, Desdemona, Emilia, *and* Attendants.

LOD.   I do beseech you, sir, trouble yourself no further.

OTH.   O, pardon me; 'twill do me good to walk.

LOD.   Madam, good night. I humbly thank your ladyship.

DES.   Your Honour is most welcome.

OTH.   Will you walk, sir?
O, Desdemona —   5

DES.   My lord?

OTH.   Get you to bed on th' instant. I will be return'd forth-
with. Dispatch your attendant there. Look't be done.

---

231 *harlotry* harlot.   236 *amaz'd* in a maze, dumbfounded [K].   239–40 *grows to
waste* is passing.   242 *satisfied* have satisfactory reasons.
    IV.III. 1 *trouble . . . further* Othello is offering to escort Lodovico to his lodg-
ings [K].   8 *Dispatch* dismiss.   11 *incontinent* immediately.   19 *stubbornness*

DES.	I will, my lord.

> *Exeunt* [Othello, Lodovico, *and* Attendants].

EMIL.	How goes it now? He looks gentler than he did.	10

DES.	He says he will return incontinent.
	He hath commanded me to go to bed,
	And bid me to dismiss you.

EMIL.	Dismiss me?

DES.	It was his bidding. Therefore, good Emilia,	
	Give me my nightly wearing, and adieu.	15
	We must not now displease him.	

EMIL.	I would you had never seen him!

DES.	So would not I. My love doth so approve him	
	That even his stubbornness, his checks, his frowns	
	(Prithee unpin me) have grace and favour in them.	20

EMIL.	I have laid those sheets you bade me on the bed.

DES.	All's one. Good faith, how foolish are our minds!
	If I do die before thee, prithee shroud me
	In one of those same sheets.

EMIL.	Come, come! You talk.

DES.	My mother had a maid call'd Barbary.	25
	She was in love; and he she lov'd prov'd mad	
	And did forsake her. She had a song of "Willow."	
	An old thing 'twas; but it express'd her fortune,	
	And she died singing it. That song to-night	
	Will not go from my mind. I have much to do	30
	But to go hang my head all at one side	
	And sing it like poor Barbary. Prithee dispatch.	

EMIL.	Shall I go fetch your nightgown?

DES.	No, unpin me here.

---

roughness. *checks* rebukes. **20** *grace and favour* something about them that I
find pleasing [K]. **22** *All's one* it is no matter. **24** *talk* talk foolishly. **26** *mad*
wild and wayward—not, insane [K]. **30-1** *I have much . . . But to* I have all I
can do to keep myself from.

	This Lodovico is a proper man.	
EMIL.	A very handsome man.	35
DES.	He speaks well.	
EMIL.	I know a lady in Venice would have walk'd barefoot to Palestine for a touch of his nether lip.	

DES.   (*sings*)
    The poor soul sat sighing by a sycamore tree,
      Sing all a green willow: 40
    Her hand on her bosom, her head on her knee,
      Sing willow, willow, willow.
    The fresh streams ran by her and murmur'd her
      moans;
      Sing Willow, willow, willow;
    Her salt tears fell from her, and soft'ned the stones.   45
      Sing willow —

Lay by these.
               willow, willow;

Prithee hie thee; he'll come anon.

    Sing all a green willow must be my garland.
    Let nobody blame him; his scorn I approve —   50

Nay, that's not next. Hark! who is't that knocks?

| EMIL. | It is the wind. | |

DES.   I call'd my love false love; but what said he then?
      Sing willow, willow, willow:
    If I court moe women, you'll couch with moe men.   55

So, get thee gone; good night. Mine eyes do itch.
Doth that bode weeping?

| EMIL. | 'Tis neither here nor there. | |

---

34 *proper* handsome. Desdemona talks idly of Lodovico to keep her mind from her troubles. There is no reason to suppose that the line has been misassigned and should be given to Emilia.   39 *The poor soul* The song is a popular ballad well known to Shakespeare's audience. It appears in various versions. In those we know the forsaken lover is a man, but Shakespeare has adapted the song to fit his play. The music may be found in Richmond Noble, SHAKESPEARE'S USE OF SONG (Oxford: The Clarendon Press, 1923), pp. 152–4. The willow was a traditional symbol of

DES. I have heard it said so. O, these men, these men!
Dost thou in conscience think — tell me, Emilia —
That there be women do abuse their husbands   60
In such gross kind?

EMIL.   There be some such, no question.

DES. Wouldst thou do such a deed for all the world?

EMIL. Why, would not you?

DES.   No, by this heavenly light!

EMIL. Nor I neither by this heavenly light. I might do't as well
i' th' dark.   65

DES. Wouldst thou do such a deed for all the world?

EMIL. The world's a huge thing. It is a great price for a small
vice.

DES. Good troth, I think thou wouldst not.

EMIL. By my troth, I think I should; and undo't when I had   70
done it. Marry, I would not do such a thing for a joint-
ring, nor for measures of lawn, nor for gowns, petticoats,
nor caps, nor any petty exhibition; but, for all the whole
world — 'Ud's pity! who would not make her husband a
cuckold to make him a monarch? I should venture purga-   75
tory for't.

DES. Beshrew me if I would do such a wrong
For the whole world.

EMIL. Why, the wrong is but a wrong i' th' world; and having
the world for your labour, 'tis a wrong in your own   80
world, and you might quickly make it right.

DES. I do not think there is any such woman.

---

unrequited love.   47 *these* probably some jewels.   55 *moe* more (not a contrac-
tion of "more" but an independent formation from the same root [ĸ]).   57 *neither
here nor there* means nothing.   59 *in conscience* with real conviction.   60 *abuse*
deceive.   61 *gross kind* obscene manner.   70 *undo't* make it right again.   71
joint-ring a ring made of separable halves, commonly used as a love token.
72 *lawn* fine linen.   73 *exhibition* offer of a gift.   74 *'Ud's pity* by God's pity (an
oath).   77 *Beshrew* curse.   81 *make it right* by your decree as ruler of the world.

EMIL. Yes, a dozen; and as many to th' vantage as would store
　　　　　the world they play'd for.
　　　　But I do think it is their husbands' faults
　　　　If wives do fall. Say that they slack their duties　　　　　85
　　　　And pour our treasures into foreign laps;
　　　　Or else break out in peevish jealousies,
　　　　Throwing restraint upon us; or say they strike us,
　　　　Or scant our former having in despite —
　　　　Why, we have galls; and though we have some grace,　　90
　　　　Yet have we some revenge. Let husbands know
　　　　Their wives have sense like them. They see, and smell,
　　　　And have their palates both for sweet and sour,
　　　　As husbands have. What is it that they do
　　　　When they change us for others? Is it sport?　　　　　95
　　　　I think it is. And doth affection breed it?
　　　　I think it doth. Is't frailty that thus errs?
　　　　It is so too. And have not we affections,
　　　　Desires for sport, and frailty, as men have?
　　　　Then let them use us well; else let them know,　　　100
　　　　The ills we do, their ills instruct us so.

DES. 　Good night, good night. Heaven me such uses send,
　　　　Not to pick bad from bad, but by bad mend!　　*Exeunt.*

---

83. *to th' vantage* to boot, in addition. *store* populate. 　84 *But I do think* Emilia
drops her jesting and speaks with some feeling. She does not, however, defend
unfaithful wives on moral grounds, but merely asserts that faithless or abusive husbands have no just ground of complaint if their wives avenge themselves by
infidelity [K]. 　87 *peevish* childish. 　88 *Throwing* inflicting. 　89 *scant . . .
despite* reduce our allowance to spite us. 　90 *galls* capacity for resentment. *grace*
virtue. 　91 *revenge* vindictiveness. 　92 *sense* feelings. 　96 *affection* desire for
pleasure [K]. 　99 *frailty* weakness of the flesh. 　102 *uses* ways, practices. 　103
Not to pick . . . bad mend that I may not let ill treatment teach me to return
evil for evil but may use it as discipline for my own improvement [K].

Act Five

<><><><><><><><><><><><><><><><><><><><><><><><><><><><><><><>

SCENE I. [*Cyprus. A street.*]

Enter Iago *and* Roderigo.

IAGO. Here, stand behind this bulk; straight will he come.
Wear thy good rapier bare, and put it home.
Quick, quick! Fear nothing; I'll be at thy elbow.
It makes us, or it mars us — think on that,
And fix most firm thy resolution.   5

ROD. Be near at hand. I may miscarry in't.

IAGO. Here, at thy hand. Be bold, and take thy stand.

                                        [*Stands aside.*]

ROD. I have no great devotion to the deed,
And yet he hath given me satisfying reasons.
'Tis but a man gone. Forth my sword! He dies!   10

IAGO. I have rubb'd this young quat almost to the sense,
And he grows angry. Now whether he kill Cassio,
Or Cassio him, or each do kill the other,
Every way makes my game. Live Roderigo,
He calls me to a restitution large   15

V.I. 1 *bulk* some structure that projected into the street from the wall of a building
—perhaps a "stall" or small shop [K]. *straight* straightway. 6 *miscarry* fail; go
wrong. Roderigo is nervous, not timid [K]. 11 *quat* contemptible youngster—
literally, pimple [K]. *to the sense* so that he feels it. The pimple has been
rubbed to the quick. 14 *makes my game* helps me win the game [K] (Q¹; F¹:
"gaine"). This reading has been much disputed. *Live Roderigo* if Roderigo
lives (the subjunctive).

Of gold and jewels that I bobb'd from him
As gifts to Desdemona.
It must not be. If Cassio do remain,
He hath a daily beauty in his life
That makes me ugly; and besides, the Moor   20
May unfold me to him; there stand I in much peril.
No, he must die. But so! I hear him coming.

Enter Cassio.

ROD.   I know his gait. 'Tis he. Villain, thou diest!

[Makes a pass at Cassio.]

CAS.   That thrust had been mine enemy indeed
But that my coat is better than thou know'st.   25
I will make proof of thine.

[Draws, and wounds Roderigo.]

ROD.   O, I am slain!

*[*Iago *rushes from his post, wounds*
Cassio *in the leg, and exit.]*

CAS.   I am maim'd for ever. Help, ho! Murder! murder!

[Falls.]

Enter Othello.

OTH.   The voice of Cassio. Iago keeps his word.

ROD.   O, villain that I am!

OTH.   It is even so.

CAS.   O, help, ho! light! a surgeon!   30

OTH.   'Tis he. O brave Iago, honest and just,
That hast such noble sense of thy friend's wrong!
Thou teachest me. Minion, your dear lies dead,
And your unblest fate hies. Strumpet, I come.
Forth of my heart those charms, thine eyes, are blotted.   35
Thy bed, lust-stain'd, shall with lust's blood be spotted.

Exit.

---

16 *bobb'd* cheated. 21 *unfold* expose. 25 *coat is better* Cassio wears a shirt of
mail under his coat [K]. 32 *sense of* feeling for. 33 *Minion* darling, Desdemona
(used with contempt). 34 *hies* quickly approaches. 35 *Forth of* from forth.

Enter Lodovico *and* Gratiano.

CAS.   What, ho? No watch? No passage? Murder! murder!

GRA.   'Tis some mischance. The cry is very direful.

CAS.   O, help!

LOD.   Hark!   40

ROD.   O wretched villain!

LOD.   Two or three groan. It is a heavy night.
         These may be counterfeits. Let's think't unsafe
         To come in to the cry without more help.

ROD.   Nobody come? Then shall I bleed to death.   45

LOD.   Hark!

Enter Iago, *with a light.*

GRA.   Here's one comes in his shirt, with light and weapons.

IAGO.   Who's there? Whose noise is this that cries on murder?

LOD.   We do not know.

IAGO.   Did not you hear a cry?

CAS.   Here, here! For heaven's sake, help me!

IAGO.   What's the matter?   50

GRA.   This is Othello's ancient, as I take it.

LOD.   The same indeed, a very valiant fellow.

IAGO.   What are you here that cry so grievously?

CAS.   Iago? O, I am spoil'd, undone by villains!
         Give me some help.   55

IAGO.   O me, Lieutenant! What villains have done this?

CAS.   I think that one of them is hereabout
         And cannot make away.

IAGO.   O treacherous villains!

---

37 *passage* passers-by.   42 *heavy* thick and cloudy.   44 *come in to* approach.
48 *cries on* cries out, shouts.   54 *spoil'd* crippled.

What are you there? Come in, and give some help.

[*To* Lodovico *and* Gratiano.]

ROD. O, help me here! 60

CAS. That's one of them.

IAGO.   O murd'rous slave! O villain!

[*Stabs* Roderigo.]

ROD. O damn'd Iago! O inhuman dog!

IAGO. Kill men i' th' dark? Where be these bloody thieves?
How silent is this town! Ho! murder! murder!
What may you be? Are you of good or evil? 65

improvises by killing Rod [handwritten note]

LOD. As you shall prove us, praise us.

IAGO. Signior Lodovico?

LOD. He, sir.

IAGO. I cry you mercy. Here's Cassio hurt by villains.

GRA. Cassio? 70

IAGO. How is it, brother?

CAS. My leg is cut in two.

IAGO.   Marry, heaven forbid!
Light, gentlemen. I'll bind it with my shirt.

Enter Bianca.

BIAN. What is the matter, ho? Who is't that cried?

IAGO. Who is't that cried? 75

BIAN. O my dear Cassio! my sweet Cassio!
O Cassio, Cassio, Cassio!

IAGO. O notable strumpet! — Cassio, may you suspect
Who they should be that thus have mangled you?

CAS. No. 80

---

66 *As you . . . praise us* value (literally, appraise) us as you find us out to be (a variation of an old proverb).   69 *cry you mercy* beg your pardon (for not recognizing you) [K].   82 *chair* kind of litter.   85 *trash* worthless creature, Bianca. 94 *accidents* sudden happenings.   95 *neglected* failed to recognize.   98 *well said*

GRA.   I am sorry to find you thus. I have been to seek you.

IAGO.   Lend me a garter. So. O for a chair
To bear him easily hence!

BIAN.   Alas, he faints! O Cassio, Cassio, Cassio!

IAGO.   Gentlemen all, I do suspect this trash   85
To be a party in this injury. —
Patience awhile, good Cassio. — Come, come!
Lend me a light. Know we this face or no?
Alas, my friend and my dear countryman
Roderigo? No. Yes, sure. O heaven! Roderigo.   90

GRA.   What, of Venice?

IAGO.   Even he, sir. Did you know him?

GRA.   Know him? Ay.

IAGO.   Signior Gratiano? I cry you gentle pardon.
These bloody accidents must excuse my manners
That so neglected you.

GRA.   I am glad to see you.   95

IAGO.   How do you, Cassio? — O, a chair, a chair!

GRA.   Roderigo?

IAGO.   He, he, 'tis he! [*A chair brought in.*] O, that's well said!
the chair.
Some good man bear him carefully from hence.
I'll fetch the General's surgeon. [*To* Bianca] For you,
mistress.   100
Save you your labour. — He that lies slain here, Cassio,
Was my dear friend. What malice was between you?

CAS.   None in the world; nor do I know the man.

IAGO.   [*to* Bianca] What, look you pale? — O, bear him out o'
th' air.   [Cassio *and* Roderigo *are borne off.*]
Stay you, good gentlemen. — Look you pale, mistress? —   105

---

well done.   101 *Save you your labour* don't trouble yourself. Bianca is attempting
to care for Cassio [K].   102 *malice* enmity.   103 *nor do I know the man* We have
already seen that Cassio was not acquainted with Roderigo (II.I.261; II.III.265–7)
[K].   105 *good gentlemen* Lodovico and Gratiano.

Do you perceive the gastness of her eye? —
Nay, an you stare, we shall hear more anon.
Behold her well; I pray you look upon her.
Do you see, gentlemen? Nay, guiltiness will speak,
Though tongues were out of use.   110

Enter Emilia.

EMIL.   'Las, what's the matter? What's the matter, husband?

IAGO.   Cassio hath here been set on in the dark
By Roderigo, and fellows that are scap'd.
He's almost slain, and Roderigo dead.

EMIL.   Alas, good gentleman! alas, good Cassio!   115

IAGO.   This is the fruit of whoring. Prithee, Emilia,
Go know of Cassio where he supp'd to-night.
[*To* Bianca] What, do you shake at that?

BIAN.   He supp'd at my house; but I therefore shake not.

IAGO.   O, did he so? I charge you go with me.   120

EMIL.   Fie, fie upon thee, strumpet!

BIAN.   I am no strumpet, but of life as honest
As you that thus abuse me.

EMIL.   As I? Foh! fie upon thee!

IAGO.   Kind gentlemen, let's go see poor Cassio dress'd.
[*To* Bianca] Come, mistress, you must tell's another
tale. —   125
Emilia, run you to the citadel
And tell my lord and lady what hath happ'd. —

---

106 *gastness* ghastly, terrified look (F¹; Q¹, Q²: "icastures" [gestures]) . Neither reading is entirely satisfactory, but F¹ seems preferable.   107 *we shall hear more* her
confession.   117 *know of* learn from.   119 *shake* with fear.   122 *honest* chaste.
124 *dress'd* have his wounds dressed.   129 *fordoes* ruins.

V.II. 1 *It is the cause* Othello has subdued his fury. He is resolved to kill Desdemona as an act of justice. "It is the cause that I must bear in mind—the guilt
that calls for the punishment of death." He will not think of his own wrongs but
solely of her offence against the right [K]. Othello's taking upon himself the power
to execute justice is the supreme point of his tragic madness; in the guise of the
impartial judge he executes the most horrible of crimes.   2 *it* her supposed un-

Will you go on afore? [*Aside*] This is the night
That either makes me or fordoes me quite.   *Exeunt.*

❖❖❖❖❖❖❖❖❖❖❖❖❖❖

SCENE II.
[*Cyprus. A bedchamber in the Castle.*]

Desdemona *in her bed. Enter* Othello *with a light.*

OTH.   It is the cause, it is the cause, my soul.
Let me not name it to you, you chaste stars!
It is the cause. Yet I'll not shed her blood,
Nor scar that whiter skin of hers than snow,
And smooth as monumental alablaster.   5
Yet she must die, else she'll betray more men.
Put out the light, and then put out the light.
If I quench thee, thou flaming minister,
I can again thy former light restore,
Should I repent me; but once put out thy light,   10
Thou cunning'st pattern of excelling nature,
I know not where is that Promethean heat
That can thy light relume. When I have pluck'd the rose,
I cannot give it vital growth again;
It needs must wither. I'll smell it on the tree.   15

He kisses her.

O balmy breath, that dost almost persuade
Justice to break her sword! One more, one more!
Be thus when thou art dead, and I will kill thee,
And love thee after. One more, and this the last!

---

chastity.   5 *alablaster* alabaster, a white translucent stone.   7 *Put out . . . the
light* extinguish the light he holds and then extinguish the light of her life.
8 *flaming minister* the torch in his hand.   10 *thy* Desdemona's.   11 *cunning'st*
most perfectly created.   *pattern . . . nature* reflection of the perfection and excellence of all creation.   12 *Promethean heat* Prometheus stole fire from heaven
to animate a clay image that he had made [K]. Only the fire of heaven can rekindle
life.   13 *relume* light again (F¹; Q¹: "returne").   17 *Justice* This makes it clear
that Othello is thinking of justice—as opposed to revenge—in line 1 [K]. The
sword and the scale were traditional emblems of justice.

So sweet was ne'er so fatal. I must weep,   20
But they are cruel tears. This sorrow's heavenly;
It strikes where it doth love. She wakes.

DES.   Who's there? Othello?

OTH.   Ay, Desdemona.

DES.   Will you come to bed, my lord?

OTH.   Have you pray'd to-night, Desdemona?

DES.   Ay, my lord.   25

OTH.   If you bethink yourself of any crime
Unreconcil'd as yet to heaven and grace,
Solicit for it straight.

DES.   Alack, my lord, what may you mean by that?

OTH.   Well, do it, and be brief; I will walk by.   30
I would not kill thy unprepared spirit.
No, heaven forfend! I would not kill thy soul.

DES.   Talk you of killing?

OTH.   Ay, I do.

DES.   Then heaven
Have mercy on me!

OTH.   Amen, with all my heart!

DES.   If you say so, I hope you will not kill me.   35

OTH.   Humh!

DES.   And yet I fear you; for you are fatal then
When your eyes roll so. Why I should fear I know not,
Since guiltiness I know not; but yet I feel I fear.

OTH.   Think on thy sins.

---

21 *cruel tears* not tears of mercy [K]. *This sorrow's heavenly* my sorrow is like
that which God feels when he punishes the guilty; he loves the sinner, yet punishes
the sin. Cf. HEBREWS, XII, 6: "Whom the Lord loveth he chasteneth." Here again
we see that Othello regards himself as the agent of divine justice. He strives to
maintain this attitude of mind throughout the scene, but in vain [K].   28 *Solicit*
pray. *straight* at once.   30 *walk by* step aside.   32 *forfend* forbid.   40 *They are*
loves . . . you I am conscious of no sin, unless it be the sin of loving you too
much. An allusion to the idea that to idolize a mortal is a sin against God [K].

DES.   They are loves I bear to you.   40

OTH.   Ay, and for that thou diest.

DES.   That death 's unnatural that kills for loving.
       Alas, why gnaw you so your nether lip?
       Some bloody passion shakes your very frame.
       These are portents; but yet I hope, I hope,   45
       They do not point on me.

OTH.   Peace and be still!

DES.   I will so. What's the matter?

OTH.   That handkerchief which I so lov'd and gave thee
       Thou gav'st to Cassio.

DES.   No, by my life and soul!
       Send for the man and ask him.

OTH.   Sweet soul, take heed,   50
       Take heed of perjury; thou art on thy deathbed.

DES.   Ay, but not yet to die.

OTH.   Yes, presently.
       Therefore confess thee freely of thy sin;
       For to deny each article with oath
       Cannot remove nor choke the strong conception   55
       That I do groan withal. Thou art to die.

DES.   Then Lord have mercy on me!

OTH.   I say amen.

DES.   And have you mercy too! I never did
       Offend you in my life; never lov'd Cassio
       But with such general warranty of heaven   60
       As I might love. I never gave him token.

OTH.   By heaven, I saw my handkerchief in's hand!

---

41 *that* love; but Othello means her love for other men.   45 *portents* ominous
signs.   47 *the matter* the real issue disturbing you.   50 *Sweet soul, take heed*
Othello masters his rising anger and becomes once more, for a moment, the com-
passionate and inexorable judge [K].   52 *presently* immediately.   54 *article* item
(in the list of sins of which he is accusing her).   55 *conception* belief, conviction.
56 *groan withal* groan with thinking of.   60 *with such . . . , heaven* with that love
for one's fellow men which heaven warrants us in feeling [K].

O perjur'd woman! thou dost stone my heart,
And mak'st me call what I intend to do
A murder, which I thought a sacrifice.   65
I saw the handkerchief.

DES.   He found it then.
I never gave it him. Send for him hither.
Let him confess a truth.

OTH.   He hath confess'd.

DES.   What, my lord?

OTH.   That he hath us'd thee.

DES.   How? unlawfully?

OTH.   Ay.   70

DES.   He will not say so.

OTH.   No, his mouth is stopp'd.
Honest Iago hath ta'en order for't.

DES.   O, my fear interprets. What, is he dead?

OTH.   Had all his hairs been lives, my great revenge
Had stomach for them all.   75

DES.   Alas, he is betray'd, and I undone!

OTH.   Out, strumpet! Weep'st thou for him to my face?

DES.   O, banish me, my lord, but kill me not!

OTH.   Down, strumpet!

DES.   Kill me to-morrow; let me live to-night!   80

OTH.   Nay, an you strive —

---

63 *stone* harden. Othello does not wish to kill her in anger, but he is afraid that
her supposed perjury is driving him to this.   65 *sacrifice* to offended justice.
72 *ta'en order* arranged.   75 *stomach* appetite, capacity.   76 *Alas . . . undone*
Desdemona means that Cassio has been the victim of some plot, and that she is
lost because his death makes it impossible for him to testify to her innocence. To
Othello, however, her words appear to be a confession of guilt. He takes her to
mean that Cassio's intrigue with her has been disclosed. Her terrified appeals for
mercy only add to his misunderstanding [K].   82 *Being done . . . pause* once the
deed of execution has begun, there is no stopping.   84 *My lord, my lord* The
effect of this sudden outcry of Emilia, who is coming with important news, is

DES.   But half an hour!

OTH.   Being done, there is no pause.

DES.   But while I say one prayer!

OTH.   It is too late.

                                He smothers her.

                    Emilia *at the door.*

EMIL.   (*calls within*) My lord, my lord! What, ho! my lord, my
            lord!

OTH.   What noise is this? Not dead? not yet quite dead?   85
            I that am cruel am yet merciful;
            I would not have thee linger in thy pain.
            So, so.

EMIL.   (*within*) What, ho! my lord, my lord!

OTH.   Who's there?

EMIL.   [*within*] O, good my lord, I would speak a word with you!   90

OTH.   Yes, 'tis Emilia. — By-and-by. — She's dead. —
            'Tis like she comes to speak of Cassio's death.
            The noise was here. Ha! no more moving?
            Still as the grave. — Shall she come in? Were't good? —
            I think she stirs again. No. — What's the best?   95
            If she come in, she'll sure speak to my wife.
            My wife! my wife! what wife? I have no wife.
            O, insupportable! O heavy hour!
            Methinks it should be now a huge eclipse
            Of sun and moon, and that th' affrighted globe   100
            Should yawn at alteration.

---

precisely like that of the knocking at the gate in MACBETH [K].   88 *So, so* With
these words Othello presses the pillow down more firmly on Desdemona's head
[K]. There is little warrant for the stage tradition, going back to Garrick, which
would have him stab her at this point.   92 *like* likely that.   93 *The noise* of a
movement on Desdemona's part [K].   97 *My wife! my wife* The full force of what
he has done for a moment overwhelms Othello.   99 *it should . . . eclipse* it
would be appropriate for an eclipse to occur now. Such heavenly phenomena were
usually seen as reflections of horror and disorder on earth.   100 *affrighted globe*
terrified earth.   101 *yawn* open wide, in an earthquake.   *at alteration* at the
dreadful change in the order of nature that such an eclipse portends [K].

EMIL.	[*within*] I do beseech you
	That I may speak with you, O good my lord!
OTH.	I had forgot thee. O, come in, Emilia.
	Soft, by-and-by. — Let me the curtains draw. —
	Where art thou? [*Opens the door.*]

Enter Emilia.

What's the matter with thee now?   105

EMIL.	O my good lord, yonder's foul murder done!
OTH.	What? now?
EMIL.	But now, my lord.
OTH.	It is the very error of the moon.
	She comes more nearer earth than she was wont 110
	And makes men mad.
EMIL.	Cassio, my lord, hath kill'd a young Venetian
	Call'd Roderigo.
OTH.	Roderigo kill'd?
	And Cassio kill'd?
EMIL.	No, Cassio is not kill'd.
OTH.	Not Cassio kill'd? Then murder's out of tune, 115
	And sweet revenge grows harsh.
DES.	O, falsely, falsely murder'd!
EMIL.	O Lord! what cry is that?
OTH.	That? What?
EMIL.	Out and alas! that was my lady's voice.
	Help! help, ho! help! O lady, speak again! 120
	Sweet Desdemona! O sweet mistress, speak!
DES.	A guiltless death I die.

109 *error* aberration, irregularity (literally, wandering from its proper sphere).
110 *nearer* F¹; Q¹, K: "near the." The F¹ reading is more idiomatic Elizabethan
English.   111 *makes men mad* Lunacy, as the word implies, was thought to be
due to the malign influence of the moon [K].   119 *Out* Originally a rallying cry;
then, often, a cry for help or an interjection of distress [K].   124 *Nobody* With
her dying breath Desdemona takes upon herself the guilt for Othello's sin.   125

EMIL.	O, who hath done this deed?
DES.	Nobody — I myself. Farewell.
	Commend me to my kind lord. O, farewell! 125

She dies.

OTH.	Why, how should she be murd'red?
EMIL.	Alas, who knows?
OTH.	You heard her say herself, it was not I.
EMIL.	She said so. I must needs report a truth.
OTH.	She's like a liar gone to burning hell!
	'Twas I that kill'd her.
EMIL.	O, the more angel she, 130
	And you the blacker devil!
OTH.	She turn'd to folly, and she was a whore.
EMIL.	Thou dost belie her, and thou art a devil.
OTH.	She was false as water.
EMIL.	Thou art rash as fire to say
	That she was false. O she was heavenly true! 135
OTH.	Cassio did top her. Ask thy husband else.
	O, I were damn'd beneath all depth in hell
	But that I did proceed upon just grounds
	To this extremity. Thy husband knew it all.
EMIL.	My husband? 140
OTH.	Thy husband.
EMIL.	That she was false to wedlock?
OTH.	Ay, with Cassio. Nay, had she been true,
	If heaven would make me such another world
	Of one entire and perfect chrysolite, 145

Commend me give my love.   132 *folly* unchastity.   133 *belie* slander.   134 *false as water* A proverbial comparison. Water takes every shape, having none of its own [K].   139 *extremity* final punishment.   140 *My husband* Emilia's astonishment, which comes out in her helpless repetition of the word, proves that she had not suspected Iago. Her denunciation of "some eternal villain" (IV.II.130*ff*.) was purely impersonal [K].   145 *chrysolite* topaz, a semiprecious stone.

I'ld not have sold her for it.

EMIL.   My husband?

OTH.   Ay, 'twas he that told me first.
An honest man he is, and hates the slime
That sticks on filthy deeds.

EMIL.   My husband?

OTH.   What needs this iterance, woman? I say, thy husband.   150

EMIL.   O mistress, villainy hath made mocks with love!
My husband say that she was false?

OTH.   He, woman.
I say, thy husband. Dost understand the word?
My friend, thy husband; honest, honest Iago.

EMIL.   If he say so, may his pernicious soul   155
Rot half a grain a day! he lies to th' heart.
She was too fond of her most filthy bargain.

OTH.   Ha!

EMIL.   Do thy worst.
This deed of thine is no more worthy heaven   160
Than thou wast worthy her.

OTH.   Peace, you were best.

EMIL.   Thou hast not half the power to do me harm
As I have to be hurt. O gull! O dolt!
As ignorant as dirt! thou hast done a deed —
I care not for thy sword; I'll make thee known,   165
Though I lost twenty lives. Help! help! O, help!
The Moor hath kill'd my mistress! Murder! murder!

                   Enter Montano, Gratiano, Iago, *and
                   others.*

MON.   What is the matter? How now, General?

---

150 *iterance* repetition.   151 *villainy hath . . . with love* some villain has be-
mocked your wife's love for you—by false evidence that she is unfaithful. Emilia
cannot yet believe that this villain is Iago. See lines 172ff. [K].   161 *you were best*
it would be best for you.   163 *to be hurt* to endure the utmost harm that you
can do me [K].   *gull* dupe.   *dolt* stupid creature.   165 *thy sword* Othello lays
his hand on his sword. We are not to suppose that he actually draws it [K].

EMIL.	O, are you come, Iago? You have done well,
	That men must lay their murders on your neck. 170
GRA.	What is the matter?
EMIL.	Disprove this villain, if thou be'st a man.
	He says thou told'st him that his wife was false.
	I know thou didst not; thou'rt not such a villain.
	Speak, for my heart is full. 175
IAGO.	I told him what I thought, and told no more
	Than what he found himself was apt and true.
EMIL.	But did you ever tell him she was false?
IAGO.	I did.
EMIL.	You told a lie, an odious damned lie! 180
	Upon my soul, a lie! a wicked lie!
	She false with Cassio? Did you say with Cassio?
IAGO.	With Cassio, mistress. Go to, charm your tongue.
EMIL.	I will not charm my tongue; I am bound to speak:
	My mistress here lies murdered in her bed — 185
ALL.	O heavens forfend!
EMIL.	And your reports have set the murder on.
OTH.	Nay, stare not, masters. It is true indeed.
GRA.	'Tis a strange truth.
MON.	O monstrous act!
EMIL.	Villainy, villainy, villainy! 190
	I think upon't, I think! I smell't! O villainy!
	I thought so then. I'll kill myself for grief.
	O villainy, villainy!
IAGO.	What, are you mad? I charge you get you home.
EMIL.	Good gentlemen, let me have leave to speak. 195

177 *apt* plausible, likely.   183 *charm* silence (as though it were spellbound).
184 *bound* in duty bound.   192 *I thought so then* An obvious reference to Emilia's
outburst in IV.II.130*ff.* What she means is not that she thought that Iago was to
blame, but merely that she had suspected "some villainy" as the cause of Othello's
suspicion [K].

'Tis proper I obey him, but not now.
Perchance, Iago, I will ne'er go home.

OTH. O! O! O!   *Falls on the bed.*

EMIL.   Nay, lay thee down and roar!
For thou hast kill'd the sweetest innocent
That e'er did lift up eye.

OTH.   O, she was foul!   [*Rises.*] 200
I scarce did know you, uncle. There lies your niece,
Whose breath, indeed, these hands have newly stopp'd.
I know this act shows horrible and grim.

GRA. Poor Desdemona! I am glad thy father's dead.
Thy match was mortal to him, and pure grief   205
Shore his old thread atwain. Did he live now,
This sight would make him do a desperate turn;
Yea, curse his better angel from his side,
And fall to reprobance.

OTH. 'Tis pitiful; but yet Iago knows   210
That she with Cassio hath the act of shame
A thousand times committed. Cassio confess'd it;
And she did gratify his amorous works
With that recognizance and pledge of love
Which I first gave her. I saw it in his hand.   215
It was a handkerchief, an antique token
My father gave my mother.

EMIL. O God! O heavenly pow'rs!

IAGO. Zounds, hold your peace!

EMIL.   'Twill out, 'twill out! I peace?
No, I will speak as liberal as the North.   220
Let heaven and men and devils, let them all,

197 *Perchance . . . go home* "I will" should not be understood as "I shall." Emilia means that, if what she suspects is true, she may refuse to live with Iago as his wife. But her words are ominous [K].   201 *you, uncle* Gratiano, Brabantio's brother.   203 *shows* appears.   206 *thread* of his life, cut by the Fate, Atrapos, with her shears.   207 *a desperate turn* some desperate act.   209 *reprobance* damnation of his soul (by driving away his "better angel") (F¹; Q¹: "reprobation" which has the same meaning and is preferred by some editors).   213 *gratify*

All, all, cry shame against me, yet I'll speak.

IAGO. Be wise, and get you home.

EMIL. I will not.

[*Iago draws and threatens* Emilia.]

GRA. Fie!
Your sword upon a woman?

EMIL. O thou dull Moor, that handkerchief thou speak'st of 225
I found by fortune, and did give my husband;
For often with a solemn earnestness
(More than indeed belong'd to such a trifle)
He begg'd of me to steal't.

IAGO. Villainous whore!

EMIL. She give it Cassio? No, alas, I found it, 230
And I did give't my husband.

IAGO. Filth, thou liest!

EMIL. By heaven, I do not, I do not, gentlemen.
O murd'rous coxcomb! what should such a fool
Do with so good a wife?

OTH. Are there no stones in heaven
But what serves for the thunder? Precious villain! 235

The Moor *runs at* Iago, [*but is disarmed by* Montano]. Iago *kills his
wife.*

GRA. The woman falls. Sure he hath kill'd his wife.

EMIL. Ay, ay. O, lay me by my mistress' side. *Exit* Iago.

GRA. He's gone, but his wife's kill'd.

MON. 'Tis a notorious villain. Take you this weapon,

---

reward. 214 *recognizance* token (literally, a legal term for a recorded obligation).
220 *liberal as the North* freely as the north wind blows. 233 *coxcomb* fool. This
use is derived from the uniform of the professional fool or jester, who wore a cap
crested with a bit of red cloth representing the comb of a cock [K]. Not all jesters,
however, were so attired. 234 *stones* thunderbolts. Has heaven no spare bolt to
smite down this villain? Is it keeping all its stones in store to discharge in thunder-
storms? [K]. 239 *notorious* notable.

Which I have here recover'd from the Moor.   240
Come, guard the door without. Let him not pass,
But kill him rather. I'll after that same villain,
For 'tis a damned slave.

> *Exeunt* Montano *and* Gratiano [*with
> others. Manent* Othello *and* Emilia].

OTH.   I am not valiant neither;
But every puny whipster gets my sword.
But why should honour outlive honesty?   245
Let it go all.

EMIL.   What did thy song bode, lady?
Hark, canst thou hear me? I will play the swan,
And die in music. [*Sings*] "Willow, willow, willow."
Moor, she was chaste; she lov'd thee, cruel Moor.
So come my soul to bliss as I speak true.   250
So speaking as I think, I die, I die.   *She dies.*

OTH.   I have another weapon in this chamber:
It is a sword of Spain, the ice-brook's temper.
O, here it is. — Uncle, I must come forth.

GRA.   (*within*) If thou attempt it, it will cost thee dear.   255
Thou hast no weapon, and perforce must suffer.

OTH.   Look in upon me then and speak with me,
Or, naked as I am, I will assault thee.

> [*Enter* Gratiano.]

GRA.   What is the matter?

OTH.   Behold, I have a weapon.
A better never did itself sustain   260

---

240 *recover'd* secured.   243 *I am not valiant neither* so my valour is gone—as well
as my good conscience. I am a coward, it seems, as well as a murderer [K].
244 *whipster* whippersnapper [K]. The exact meaning of the term is uncertain,
although it is clear that it is contemptuous.   245 *honour outlive honesty* reputation, the external signs of honour, outlive true honourable behaviour.   247-8 *swan
... music* The swan was reputed to sing just one song in its lifetime, and that
one immediately before death.   253 *sword of Spain* Toledo and Bilbao in Spain
were famous for the excellence of their swords.   *ice-brook's temper* tempered in
ice-cold water, as the finest swords were treated.   256 *suffer* suffer death.   258
naked unarmed.   264 *your stop* what you can stop.   267 *butt* in archery, the

Upon a soldier's thigh. I have seen the day
That with this little arm and this good sword
I have made my way through more impediments
Than twenty times your stop. But O vain boast!
Who can control his fate? 'Tis not so now.   265
Be not afraid, though you do see me weapon'd.
Here is my journey's end, here is my butt,
And very seamark of my utmost sail.
Do you go back dismay'd? 'Tis a lost fear.
Man but a rush against Othello's breast,   270
And he retires. Where should Othello go?
Now, how dost thou look now? O ill-starr'd wench!
Pale as thy smock! When we shall meet at compt,
This look of thine will hurl my soul from heaven,
And fiends will snatch at it. Cold, cold, my girl?   275
Even like thy chastity. — O cursed slave!
Whip me, ye devils,
From the possession of this heavenly sight!
Blow me about in winds! roast me in sulphur!
Wash me in steep-down gulfs of liquid fire!   280
O Desdemona, Desdemona! dead!
O! O! O!

> *Enter* Lodovico, Montano, Iago [*as
> prisoner,*] *and* Officers; Cassio *in a
> chair.*

LOD.   Where is this rash and most unfortunate man?

OTH.   That's he that was Othello. Here I am.

LOD.   Where is that viper? Bring the villain forth.   285

---

structure on which the target is placed; hence the farthest limit of the arrow's
flight.   268 *seamark* a beacon, or any other object by which a mariner checks
his course.   *utmost sail* the farthest I can sail.   269 *lost fear* wasted fear—you
have no reason to fear me [K].   270 *Man* wield or point.   *rush* bulrush, reed—the
slightest possible weapon to be used as a spear.   272 *ill-starr'd* unfortunate,
plagued by malicious stars.   *wench* used as a term of endearment.   273 *at compt*
at the last judgment, when all accounts must be settled.   274 *look of thine . . .
heaven* Othello now sees damnation as just punishment for his crime.   279–80
Blow me . . . liquid fire traditional pains of hell which appear often in medieval
and Renaissance literature.

OTH.　I look down towards his feet — but that's a fable.
　　　If that thou be'st a devil, I cannot kill thee.

　　　　　　　　　　　　　　　[*Wounds* Iago.]

LOD.　Wrench his sword from him.　　[Othello *is disarmed.*]

IAGO.　　　　　　　　　　I bleed, sir, but not kill'd.

OTH.　I am not sorry neither. I'ld have thee live;
　　　For in my sense, 'tis happiness to die.　　　　　　　290

LOD.　O thou Othello that wert once so good,
　　　Fall'n in the practice of a damned slave,
　　　What shall be said to thee?

OTH.　　　　　　　　　　　Why, anything:
　　　An honourable murderer, if you will;
　　　For naught did I in hate, but all in honour.　　　　295

LOD.　This wretch hath part confess'd his villainy.
　　　Did you and he consent in Cassio's death?

OTH.　Ay.

CAS.　Dear General, I never gave you cause.

OTH.　I do believe it, and I ask your pardon.　　　　　　300
　　　Will you, I pray, demand that demi-devil
　　　Why he hath thus ensnar'd my soul and body?

IAGO.　Demand me nothing. What you know, you know.
　　　From this time forth I never will speak word.

LOD.　What, not to pray?

GRA.　　　　　　　　　Torments will ope your lips.　　305

OTH.　Well, thou dost best.

LOD.　Sir, you shall understand what hath befall'n,
　　　Which, as I think, you know not. Here is a letter

---

286 *I look . . . his feet* to see if they are cloven, like the feet of Satan [K].
290 *sense* opinion.　292 *in the practice* through the machinations.　297 *consent
in* agree upon.　301 *demi-devil* not a devil (line 287), but a creature who is half-
devil—human in shape, but a fiend in his nature [K].　305 *ope your lips* force
you to confess. We may be sure that no torture will subdue Iago's resolution [K].
306 *thou dost best* for thy crime is unspeakable [K].　313 *gross* flagrant, monstrous.　314 *discontented paper* letter expressing dissatisfaction.　317 *belike*
probably.　*nick* nick of time (Q¹; F¹, K: "interim"). The F¹ word is a sophistication

Found in the pocket of the slain Roderigo;
And here another. The one of them imports   310
The death of Cassio to be undertook
By Roderigo.

OTH.   O villain!

CAS.   Most heathenish and most gross!

LOD.   Now here's another discontented paper
Found in his pocket too; and this, it seems,   315
Roderigo meant t' have sent this damned villain;
But that, belike, Iago in the nick
Came in and satisfied him.

OTH.   O thou pernicious caitiff! —
How came you, Cassio, by that handkerchief
That was my wife's?

CAS.   I found it in my chamber;   320
And he himself confess'd but even now
That there he dropp'd it for a special purpose
Which wrought to his desire.

OTH.   O fool! fool! fool!

CAS.   There is besides in Roderigo's letter,
How he upbraids Iago that he made him   325
Brave me upon the watch; whereon it came
That I was cast; and even but now he spake,
After long seeming dead — Iago hurt him,
Iago set him on.

LOD.   You must forsake this room and go with us.   330
Your power and your command is taken off,
And Cassio rules in Cyprus. For this slave,
If there be any cunning cruelty

---

which, in fact, renders the line unmetrical.   **318** *Came in* interposed.   *caitiff* wretch.   **323** *wrought to his desire* worked out in accordance with his wishes [K]. **326** *Brave* insult. *whereon it came* because of which it happened.   **327** *cast* dismissed.   **328** *hurt* wounded.   **333** *cunning cruelty* Shakespeare is true to Continental custom. According to Roman law torture was inflicted to extort confession. Such was also the rule in Scotland—not, however, in England, though the English often adopted the foreign custom in this regard [K].

> That can torment him much and hold him long,
> It shall be his. You shall close prisoner rest   335
> Till that the nature of your fault be known
> To the Venetian state. Come, bring away.

OTH.   Soft you! a word or two before you go.
> I have done the state some service, and they know't —
> No more of that. I pray you, in your letters,   340
> When you shall these unlucky deeds relate,
> Speak of me as I am. Nothing extenuate,
> Nor set down aught in malice. Then must you speak
> Of one that lov'd not wisely, but too well;
> Of one not easily jealous, but, being wrought,   345
> Perplex'd in the extreme; of one whose hand
> (Like the base Indian) threw a pearl away
> Richer than all his tribe; of one whose subdu'd eyes,
> Albeit unused to the melting mood,
> Drop tears as fast as the Arabian trees   350
> Their med'cinable gum. Set you down this;
> And say besides that in Aleppo once,
> Where a malignant and a turban'd Turk
> Beat a Venetian and traduc'd the state,
> I took by th' throat the circumcised dog   355
> And smote him — thus.   *He stabs himself.*

LOD.   O bloody period!

GRA.   All that's spoke is marr'd.

OTH.   I kiss'd thee ere I kill'd thee. No way but this —
> Killing myself, to die upon a kiss.

---

335 *rest* remain.   338 *Soft you* wait a moment.   342 *extenuate* diminish, tone down (not "excuse").   345 *not easily jealous* not naturally prone to suspicion. Othello refers to his general temperament—not especially to the present case. Shakespeare certainly means us to believe him. His words accord with Iago's testimony (I.III.391-2) [K]. *wrought* worked upon.   347 *Indian* Q¹; F¹: "Iudean" [Judean]. This reading has been much disputed. Kittredge, who preferred Q¹, pointed out that "the supposed ignorance of savages with regard to the value of precious stones had become proverbial." Those who prefer F¹ hold that the reference is to Judas Iscariot the betrayer of Christ (thus supporting the Christ-symbolism of Desdemona) or to Herod who, in a fit of jealousy, rejected Miriamne.   348 *subdu'd* overcome by emotion.   349 *melting mood* weeping.   350 *Arabian trees* Pliny, NATURAL HISTORY, XII, 25, 54, lines 1-18, had described the aromatic treasures of Arabia.   352 *Aleppo* city in Turkey where Venetians were allowed

He [falls upon the bed and] dies.

CAS. This did I fear, but thought he had no weapon;   360
For he was great of heart.

LOD.   O Spartan dog,
More fell than anguish, hunger, or the sea!
Look on the tragic loading of this bed.
This is thy work. The object poisons sight;
Let it be hid. Gratiano, keep the house,   365
And seize upon the fortunes of the Moor,
For they succeed on you. To you, Lord Governor,
Remains the censure of this hellish villain.
The time, the place, the torture — O, enforce it!
Myself will straight aboard, and to the state   370
This heavy act with heavy heart relate.   *Exeunt omnes.*

special trading privileges but where it was death for a Christian to strike a Turk.
Othello thus risked his life for Venice.   354 *traduc'd* insulted.   356 *thus* A stage
direction indicating that at this point Othello stabs himself.   357 *period* conclusion. *All that's . . . marr'd* Othello's fine speech has been spoiled by this
bloody peroration.   361 *Spartan dog* The allusion seems to be both to the
ferocity of the hounds of Sparta and to the traditional stony calmness of the
Spartans themselves [K].   362 *fell* fierce, cruel. *anguish* physical pain.   363 *load-*
ing F¹; Q¹: "lodging" is supported by some editors.   365 *Let it be hid* At this, no
doubt, a curtain is drawn, shutting the bed from sight of the audience [K].
367 *succeed on* descend on. *you* Gratiano, since he is Desdemona's uncle and
Othello has no heirs.   368 *censure* judgment.   370 *straight* straightway.   371
heavy sorrowful.